PART 1
ABSOLUTE BEGINNER

Rex Jones

You Must Learn VBScript for QTP/UFT

Don't Ignore The Language For Functional Automation Testing

Free Webinars, Videos, and Live Training

Mr. Jones plans to have **free** step-by-step demonstration webinars, videos, and live trainings walking people through concepts of QTP/UFT and Selenium from A - Z. The material will teach/train individuals the fundamentals of the programming language, fundamentals of QTP/UFT and Selenium, and important concepts of QTP/UFT and Selenium. All of the webinars, videos, and live training will be directed toward beginners as well as mid-level automation engineers.

Sign Up to Receive

1. 3 Tips To Master QTP/UFT Within 30 Days
   http://tinyurl.com/3-Tips-For-QTP-UFT

2. 3 Tips To Master Selenium Within 30 Days
   http://tinyurl.com/3-Tips-For-Selenium

3. Free Webinars, Videos, and Live Trainings
   http://tinyurl.com/Free-QTP-UFT-Selenium

Skype: rex.jones34
Twitter: @RexJonesII
Email: Rex.Jones@Test4Success.org
LinkedIn: https://www.linkedin.com/in/rexjones34

Rex Jones' Contact Information

Email Address: Rex.Jones@Test4Success.org
LinkedIn: https://www.linkedin.com/in/rexjones34
Books: http://tinyurl.com/Rex-Allen-Jones-Books
Twitter: @RexJonesII
Skype: rex.jones34

Table of Contents

3 Tips To Master QTP/UFT Within 30 Days
http://tinyurl.com/3-Tips-For-QTP-UFT

Free Webinars, Videos, and Live Trainings
http://tinyurl.com/Free-QTP-UFT-Selenium

Preface

I must admit, it was a challenge writing this VBScript for QTP/UFT book. The challenge stems from an unlimited access to information on the internet. All of the information in this book can be found scattered throughout search engines, blogs, etc. However, if you are searching for one consolidated resource, then this is the book for you.

Target Audience

The target audience is beginners and mid-level automation engineers. Beginners are people new to QTP/UFT who need to learn more than the basics of VBScript. Mid-level automation engineers are people with knowledge of VBScript, but want to refresh their programming skills. No prior knowledge of VBScript or programming concepts is required. However, a common myth regarding QTP/UFT is that development skills are not necessary. The truth is development skills are very necessary.

Why learn VBScript?

Can you imagine traveling to a foreign country and trying to communicate with the native people without learning their language? That is similar to communicating with QTP/UFT without learning VBScript. The purpose of this book is to help automation engineers understand that QTP/UFT cannot be fully optimized without a strong foundation of VBScript. A mistake most QTP/UFT books and training courses make is not providing solid information on the VBScript programming language. These books and training courses focus solely on QTP/UFT, which leads to automation engineers struggling with automation projects. Automation is the future of testing applications. Take this opportunity to learn VBScript.

3 Tips To Master QTP/UFT Within 30 Days
http://tinyurl.com/3-Tips-For-QTP-UFT

Free Webinars, Videos, and Live Trainings
http://tinyurl.com/Free-QTP-UFT-Selenium

About the Author

Rex Allen Jones II is a QA/Software Tester with a passion for sharing knowledge about testing software. He has been watching webinars, attending seminars, and testing applications since February 2005. Mr. Jones graduated from DeVry University in June 1999 with a Bachelor's of Science degree in Computer Information Systems (CIS).

Currently, Rex is a Sr. Consultant and former Board of Director for User Group: Dallas / Fort Worth Mercury User Group (DFWMUG) and member of User Group: Dallas / Fort Worth Quality Assurance Association (DFWQAA). In addition to his User Group memberships, he is a Certified Software Tester Engineer (CSTE) and has a Test Management Approach (TMap) certification.

Mr. Jones' advice for people interested in Functional Automation Testing is to learn the programming language. This advice led him to write 4 programming books "(Part 1 & Part 2) You Must Learn VBScript for QTP/UFT" and "(Part 1 & Part 2) Java 4 Selenium

Skype: rex.jones34
Twitter: @RexJonesII
Email: Rex.Jones@Test4Success.org
LinkedIn: https://www.linkedin.com/in/rexjones34

WebDriver". VBScript is the programming language for Unified Functional Testing (UFT) formerly known as Quick Test Professional (QTP) and Java is one of the programming languages for Selenium WebDriver.

3 Tips To Master QTP/UFT Within 30 Days
http://tinyurl.com/3-Tips-For-QTP-UFT

Free Webinars, Videos, and Live Trainings
http://tinyurl.com/Free-QTP-UFT-Selenium

About the Editor

When Samantha Mann is not improving the contents of a document through constructive editing marks and remarks, she is enjoying life as a professional in Dallas, Texas. Samantha is a User Experience guru in the realms of research and design, and works as an Information Technology consultant. Outside of work her hobbies include the typical nerd-type fun of freelance editing, reading, writing, and binge watching Netflix with her pitbull.

Connect with Samantha:

Samantha.danae.mann@gmail.com

https://www.linkedin.com/pub/samantha-mann/84/9b7/100

Skype: rex.jones34
Twitter: @RexJonesII
Email: Rex.Jones@Test4Success.org
LinkedIn: https://www.linkedin.com/in/rexjones34

Copyright, Legal Notice, and Disclaimer

This publication is protected under the US Copyright Act of 1976. All rights are reserved including resale rights which applies to international, federal, state, and local laws. The purchaser is not allowed to share or sell this book to anyone.

Please note that much of this publication is based on personal experience and anecdotal evidence. The author has made every reasonable attempt to produce accurate content in this book. He assumes no responsibility for unknown errors or omissions. Therefore, the purchaser should use this information as he/she sees fit.

Any trademarks, service marks, product names or named features are assumed to be the property of their respective owners and used only for reference.

Copyright © 2015 Test 4 Success, LLC. All rights reserved worldwide.

ISBN-13: 978-1523262267
ISBN-10: 1523262265

3 Tips To Master QTP/UFT Within 30 Days
http://tinyurl.com/3-Tips-For-QTP-UFT

Free Webinars, Videos, and Live Trainings
http://tinyurl.com/Free-QTP-UFT-Selenium

Acknowledgements

I would like to express my gratitude to my wife Tiffany, children Olivia Rexe' and Rex III, editor Samantha Mann, family, friends, and the many people who provided encouragement. Writing this book took time and your support helped pushed this book forward.

Thank You,

Rex Allen Jones II

Rex Allen Jones II

Skype: rex.jones34
Twitter: @RexJonesII
Email: Rex.Jones@Test4Success.org
LinkedIn: https://www.linkedin.com/in/rexjones34

Chapter 1 Introduction to VBScript

Overview

VBScript's full name is Microsoft Visual Basic Scripting Edition language. It is a simplified version of the Visual Basic (VB) and Visual Basic for Applications (VBA) family of programming languages. VBScript's syntax is based on Visual Basic's syntax. Syntax is a set of rules that determine how the language will be written and interpreted by the browser or server. Most of VBScript's features are taken from Visual Basic. Features, such as the control flows, operators, and procedures, are acceptable in the family of Visual Basic.

Visual Basic is the full-blown programming language, while VBScript is the scaled down version that supports scripts. Processing is the main difference between a full-blown programming language and a scripting language. A scripting language has to reprocess every time it is run, but a full-blown programming language runs faster because it is only processed one time.

VBScript is written for a runtime environment that can interpret and automate tasks. It uses the Component Object Model to access elements of the environment within which it is running. Software applications, web pages within a browser, the shells of an operating system (OS), and embedded systems are example environments that can be automated. VBScript can be used in the following instances:

- Windows administrative tasks
- HTML pages, as a client-side scripting language
- Server-side scripting language, in native Application Service Provider (ASP) pages with Internet Information Services (IIS) web server
- Embedded applications

3 Tips To Master QTP/UFT Within 30 Days
http://tinyurl.com/3-Tips-For-QTP-UFT

Free Webinars, Videos, and Live Trainings
http://tinyurl.com/Free-QTP-UFT-Selenium

- Scripting language in Quick Test Professional (QTP)/Unified Functional Testing (UFT) for automation testing

QTP/UFT uses VBScript as the scripting language for developing test scripts. An understanding of VBScript will help create and maintain test scripts in QTP/UFT.

This chapter provides general principles rather than details about the building blocks of VBScript for QTP/UFT, and will explain the following:

- ✓ Variables
- ✓ Flow Control
- ✓ Coding Standards

Variables

Variables are storage locations in memory *(see Variables and Data Types in Chapter 2.)* Scripts use variables to store data for later use. The data stored in a variable can be anything—a small number, a large number, a word, or a combination of numbers and letters (alphanumeric characters). A variable must have a good name that clearly defines its goal. Each variable must serve one purpose and not be used throughout the script for multiple purposes.

Flow Control

Code executes in a certain hierarchal order when running a script. The order of code execution is called a flow *(see Flow Control in Chapter 5.)* Simple scripts execute from the top to bottom, also known as top-down programs. The script engine begins execution with the first statement, then moves to the next statement, and continues down the script until reaching the last statement. Execution occurs in this manner when it does not include branching or looping.

Branching

Branching is a technique that causes specific statements to be executed depending on certain conditions *(see Branching Constructs in Chapter 5 Flow Control.)* VBScript has two branching constructs: The "If" branch and the "Select Case" branch.

If Branch

- If Statement: Executes a set of code when a condition is true

Figure 1.1

```
Option Explicit
Dim strTest4Success

strTest4Success = "Test 4 Success has Free Live Training and Free Valuable Videos"

If strTest4Success <> Empty Then
    MsgBox strTest4Success
End If
```

```
Option Explicit
Dim strTest4Success

strTest4Success = "Test 4 Success has Free Live Training and Free Valuable Videos"

If strTest4Success <> Empty Then
   MsgBox strTest4Success
End If
```

The output displays "Test 4 Success has Free Live Training and Free Valuable Videos."

Figure 1.2

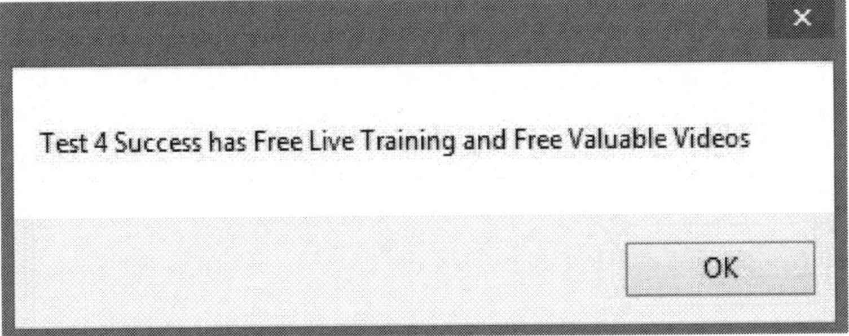

- If-Then-Else Statement: Selects one of two sets of lines to execute

Figure 1.3

```
Option Explicit
Dim strTest4Success

strTest4Success = "Test 4 Success has Free Live Training and Free Valuable Videos"

If strTest4Success = Empty Then
        MsgBox strTest4Success
Else
        MsgBox "Test 4 Success is empty"
End If
```

```
Option Explicit
Dim strTest4Success

strTest4Success = "Test 4 Success has Free Live Training and Free Valuable Videos"

If strTest4Success = Empty Then
    MsgBox strTest4Success
Else
    MsgBox "Test 4 Success is empty"
End If
```

The output displays "Test 4 Success is empty."

Figure 1.4

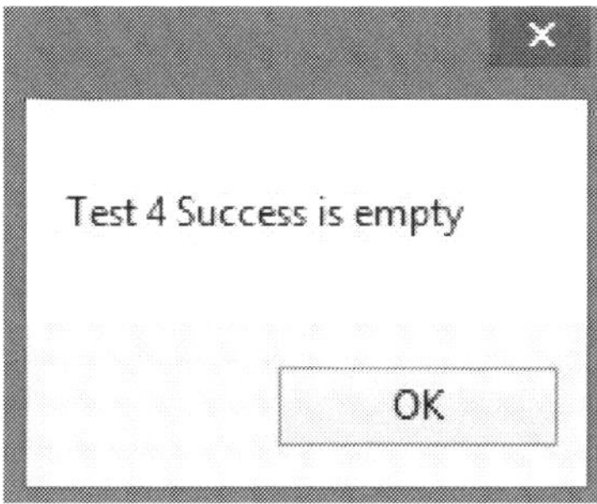

- If-Then-ElseIf Statement: Selects one of many sets of lines to execute

Figure 1.5

```
Option Explicit
Dim strMsg

strMsg = "VBScript and QTP / UFT"

If strMsg = "VBScript" Then
    MsgBox "You can master VBScript"
ElseIf strMsg = "QTP / UFT" Then
    MsgBox "You can master QTP / UFT"
ElseIf strMsg = "VBScript and QTP / UFT" Then
    MsgBox "You can master VBScript and QTP / UFT"
Else
    MsgBox "Every master was once a disaster"
End If
```

```
Option Explicit
Dim strMsg

strMsg = "VBScript and QTP / UFT"

If strMsg = "VBScript" Then
   MsgBox "You can master VBScript"
ElseIf strMsg = "QTP / UFT" Then
   MsgBox "You can master QTP / UFT"
ElseIf strMsg = "VBScript and QTP / UFT" Then
   MsgBox "You can master VBScript and QTP / UFT"
Else
   MsgBox "Every master was once a disaster"
End If
```

The output displays “You can master VBScript and QTP / UFT.”

Figure 1.6

Select Case Branch

- Select Case Statement: Makes a decision based on the actual value, not True or False. The Select Case Statement selects one of many sets of lines to execute for the same expression.

Figure 1.7

```
Option Explicit
Dim strMsg

strMsg = "VBScript and QTP / UFT"

Select Case strMsg
    Case "VBScript"
        MsgBox "You can master VBScript"
    Case "QTP / UFT"
        MsgBox "You can master QTP / UFT"
    Case "VBScript and QTP / UFT"
        MsgBox "You can master VBScript and QTP / UFT"
    Case Else
        MsgBox "Every master was once a disaster"
End Select
```

```
Option Explicit
Dim strMsg

strMsg = "VBScript and QTP / UFT"

Select Case strMsg
  Case "VBScript"
    MsgBox "You can master VBScript"
  Case "QTP / UFT"
    MsgBox "You can master QTP / UFT"
  Case "VBScript and QTP / UFT"
    MsgBox "You can master VBScript and QTP / UFT"
  Case Else
    MsgBox "Every master was once a disaster"
End Select
```

3 Tips To Master QTP/UFT Within 30 Days
http://tinyurl.com/3-Tips-For-QTP-UFT

Free Webinars, Videos, and Live Trainings
http://tinyurl.com/Free-QTP-UFT-Selenium

The output displays "You can master VBScript and QTP / UFT."

Figure 1.8

Looping

Looping executes lines of code over and over again *(see Looping Statements in Chapter 5 Flow Control.)* Looping is useful when repeating a block of code until a condition is True or False or when repeating a block of code a definite number of times. Most programmers use the following looping constructs: "For Next" and "Do Loop."

For Next

- For Next Statement: Runs the code a specified number of times

Figure 1.9

```
Option Explicit
Dim i

For i = 1 to 3
    MsgBox "Number " & i
Next
```

Skype: rex.jones34
Twitter: @RexJonesII
Email: Rex.Jones@Test4Success.org
LinkedIn: https://www.linkedin.com/in/rexjones34

```
Option Explicit
Dim i

For i = 1 to 3
   MsgBox "Number " & i
Next
```

The first output displays “Number 1,” the second output displays “Number 2,” and the third output displays “Number 3.”

Figure 1.10

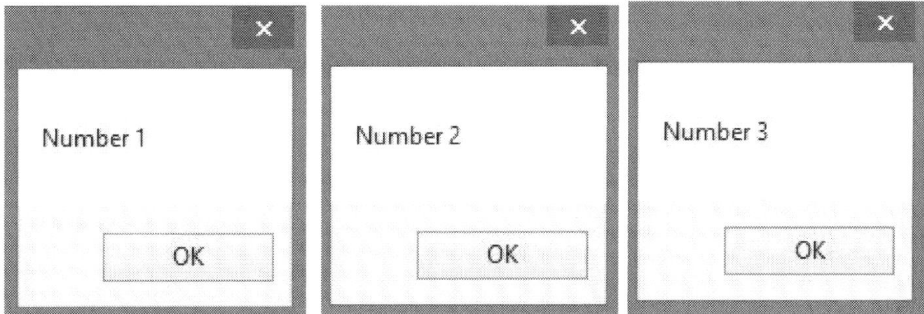

- For Each-Next Statement: Runs the code for each item in a collection (which stores a group of data) or an array (which is a matrix of data)

Figure 1.11

```
Option Explicit
Dim i
Dim intAge

intAge = Array(34, 36, 38)

For Each i In intAge
    MsgBox "Age: " & i
Next
```

Option Explicit
Dim i
Dim intAge

intAge = **Array**(34, 36, 38)

For Each i **In** intAge
   MsgBox "Age: " & i
Next

The first output displays "Age: 34," the second output displays "Age: 36," and the third output displays "Age: 38."

Skype: rex.jones34
Twitter: @RexJonesII
Email: Rex.Jones@Test4Success.org
LinkedIn: https://www.linkedin.com/in/rexjones34

Figure 1.12

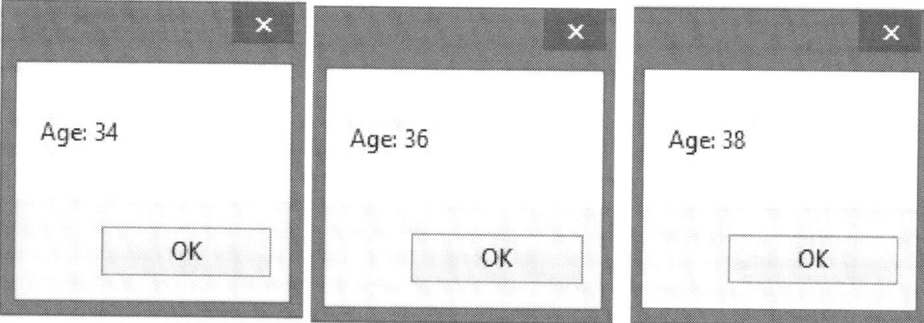

Do Loop

- Do Loop Statement: Executes the code in a loop while or until a condition is true

Figure 1.13

```
Option Explicit
Dim i

i = 1

Do While i < 3
    MsgBox "Number " & i & " is less than 3"
    i = i + 1
Loop
```

Option Explicit
Dim i

i = 1

```
Do While i < 3
   MsgBox "Number " & i & " is less than 3"
   i = i + 1
Loop
```

The first output displays "Number 1 is less than 3" and the second output displays "Number 2 is less than 3."

Figure 1.14

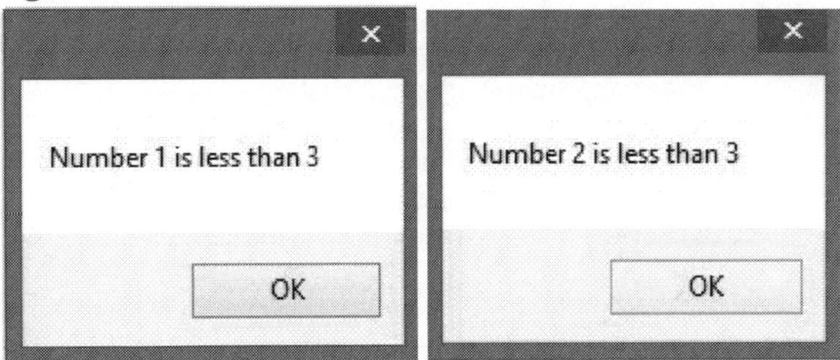

Figure 1.15

```
Option Explicit
Dim i

i = 1

Do
    MsgBox i & " is less than or equal to 3"
    i = i + 1
Loop Until i > 3
```

```
Option Explicit
Dim i
```

Skype: rex.jones34
Twitter: @RexJonesII
Email: Rex.Jones@Test4Success.org
LinkedIn: https://www.linkedin.com/in/rexjones34

```
i = 1

Do
   MsgBox i & " is less than or equal to 3"
   i = i + 1
Loop Until i > 3
```

The first output displays "1 is less than or equal to 3," the second output displays "2 is less than or equal to 3," and the third output displays "3 is less than or equal to 3."

Figure 1.16

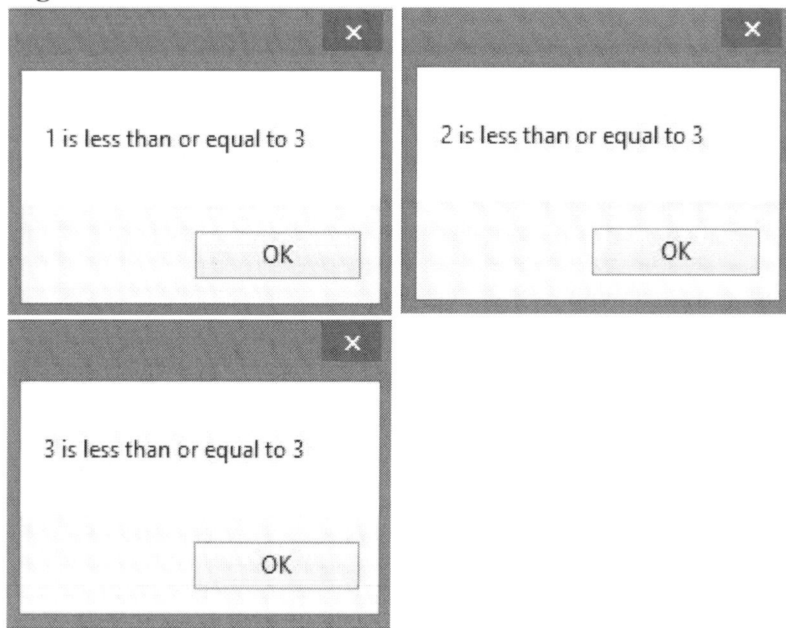

Coding Standards

It is important to practice good programming habits, because good programming habits ensures code will be easier to read, understand, and modify, as well as contain fewer bugs. This will pay off in the long run. Properly laid out code improves the readability for you and your fellow Programmers. Indentations of the lines show a subordination/hierarchical relationship to other lines of code. Accordingly, related code should be kept together on consecutive lines while separating unrelated code with a blank line.

Hungarian Naming Convention

The Hungarian Naming Convention involves giving variable names a prefix (see *Hungarian Naming Convention in Chapter 2 Variables and Data Types*.) As a result, the prefix indicates what the scope and data type of the variable are intended to be. It makes programs easier to write and read. For example, “strName” is a Hungarian Naming Convention. The prefix “str” defines the variable as a string.

Explicit Over Implicit

Programmers must be wary of using too many generic variable names (i.e., “i,” “x,” “y,” and “z”) and function names (i.e., “Function1,” “Function2,” and “Function3”). Instead, make the variable and function names explicit so the purpose is clear. Good function names are longer than good variable names. It is best to have verb-noun conventions when naming a function. For example, “GetCarModel” is a good function name. This function informs a fellow programmer reading the code that it will get the model of a car.

Comments

Code should be as self-documenting as possible. Nevertheless, it is difficult to ensure 100% self-documented code. The programmer uses comments to make the code clearer. However, there is a difference between bad comments and good comments. Bad comments clutter the overall script with excessive information that explains how the code works. The comments are excessive because the code already tells how the Sub Procedure works. A good comment answers two questions:

1. What is the purpose of the code?
2. Why did the programmer write the code?

The following is an example of a bad comment and a good comment:

Figure 1.17

```
'(Bad Comment) String "strName" combines the First Name and Last Name
strName = strFirstName & " " & strLastName

'(Good Comment) Purpose of "strName" is to place the name in the Customer table not Employee table
strName = strFirstName & " " & strLastName
```

'(Bad Comment) String "strName" combines the First Name and Last Name
strName = strFirstName & " " & strLastName

'(Good Comment) Purpose of "strName" is to place the name in the Customer table not Employee table
strName = strFirstName & " " & strLastName

Code Modularization

As more code is added to scripts, it becomes harder to read in one chunk. At some point, decisions will redirect the code by way of branching or loops. Consequently, the code gets more complex, making the introduction of errors easy. Poor layout of the code (also known as spaghetti code) makes things harder to find and fix.

Modularization is a technique programmers use to manage the code's complexity. It is the process of organizing code into modules, which can be considered building blocks. Procedures are used to achieve modularity. There are two types of procedures: Sub Procedure and Function Procedure.

3 Tips To Master QTP/UFT Within 30 Days
http://tinyurl.com/3-Tips-For-QTP-UFT

Free Webinars, Videos, and Live Trainings
http://tinyurl.com/Free-QTP-UFT-Selenium

Sub Procedure

Sub Procedure is a series of statements surrounded by the Sub and End Sub statements *(see Sub Procedure in Chapter 6 Procedures-Functions.)* It can perform an action and take arguments (also known as parameters), but does not return a value. Actions carry out a task, such as adding numbers. Arguments are special variables used for procedures to provide data as input. The following is the syntax for a Sub Procedure:

Syntax

Sub NameOfSubProcedure()
code
End Sub

Sub NameOfSubProcedure ([Argument1], [ArgumentN])
code
End Sub

Function Procedure

Function Procedure is a series of statements surrounded by the Function and End Function Statements *(see Function Procedure in Chapter 6 Procedures-Functions.)* It can perform an action, take arguments, and return a value. The value is returned by assigning a value to its name. The following is the syntax for a Function Procedure:

Syntax

Function NameOfFunctionProcedure()
code
NameOfFunctionProcedure = some value
End Function

Function NameOfFunctionProcedure ([Argument1], [ArgumentN])
code
NameOfFunctionProcedure = some value

End Function

Chapter 1 outlines the foundational principles of variables, flow control, and coding standards. Chapter 2 will explore variables and the Hungarian Naming Convention, as well the variable data types.

Chapter 2
Variables and Data Types

Variables are extremely important in VBScript. Variables hold data for the scripts. Every input, output, and process within the scripts use variables. Data within variables can be held for later use, while some variables are discarded as soon as they are used. Placing values into variables is called initializing. Values are placed into variables by default or from the application. The database is also used to store values within variables. The database could be a text file, an excel file, etc.

This chapter will explain the following:

✓ Variable Rules
✓ Variable Types
✓ Variable Lifetime/Scope
✓ Declare Variables
✓ Option Explicit
✓ Data Types
✓ Hungarian Naming Convention

Variable Rules

Variables can be used to hold values (x=3) or expressions (x = y + z). Make sure that the variable name is on the left and values are on the right when assigning values to variables. A variable can have a short name like "z" or a descriptive name like "strTestPage." The following are some rules for variables:

1) Cannot exceed 255 characters
2) Underscore "_" is the only valid non-alphanumeric character

3) Must start with a letter (uppercase or lowercase)

Variable Types

There are three types of variables. The following is a list of each variable type:

1. Scalar
2. Array
3. Constant

Scalar

Scalar variables contain only one value that can change before or during execution. The following example has a variable called "x," with a value of "34."

```
Dim x
x = 34
```

Array

Array variables contain multiple values *(see Arrays in Chapter 4.)* The following example has a variable called "y" with a size of three, which stores four values.

```
Dim y(3)

y(0) = 4
y(1) = 2
y(2) = 6
y(3) = 8
```

3 Tips To Master QTP/UFT Within 30 Days
http://tinyurl.com/3-Tips-For-QTP-UFT

Free Webinars, Videos, and Live Trainings
http://tinyurl.com/Free-QTP-UFT-Selenium

Constant

Constant variables contain values that cannot change before or during execution. The following example has a variable called "NUMBER," with a value of "3" that will not change during execution.

Const NUMBER = 3

Generally, due to an accepted convention, the name of a constant is in all capital letters. Programmers can also declare multiple constants on one line, as follows:

Const NUMBER = 3, NUMBER = 4

Literals

A literal is static (fixed) data that contains text, numbers, dates, or Boolean values. Boolean values hold values that can be True or False. Values such as True or False are literals that is not stored in a variable. However, a literal can also be stored in a variable. The following is an example of a literal:

```
Option Explicit
Dim datBirthday

datBirthday = #05/09/12#
MsgBox "Test For Success birthday is " & datBirthday
```

The output displays "Test For Success birthday is 5/9/2012"

Figure 2.1

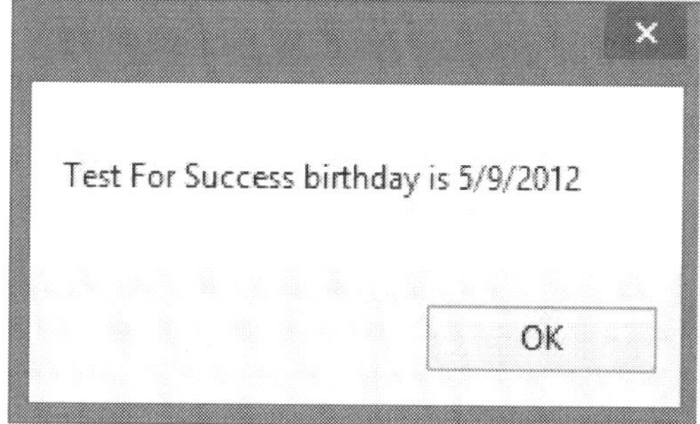

Variable Lifetime/Scope

The lifetime of a variable depends on its existence. It can exist locally or globally. Local variables are declared within a procedure, while global variables are declared outside of a procedure. A procedure is a group of code lines in a script file that perform a specific task. When a Programmer declares a variable within a procedure, then the variable can only be accessed within that procedure. The variable is destroyed after the procedure exit. Exiting a procedure occurs when the procedure terminates or returns a value to the calling code. Local variables can have the same name in different procedures, because each variable is only recognized by that specific procedure. The following is an example of two procedures (Sub and Function) possessing a local variable with the same name:

Figure 2.2

```
Option Explicit

Call DisplayOldCarColor
MsgBox "My new car is " & ReturnNewCarColor

Sub DisplayOldCarColor

    Dim strCarColor
    strCarColor = "blue"
    MsgBox "My old car was " & strCarColor

End Sub

Function ReturnNewCarColor

    Dim strCarColor
    strCarColor = "black"
    ReturnNewCarColor = strCarColor

End Function
```

Option Explicit

Call DisplayOldCarColor
MsgBox "My new car is" & ReturnNewCarColor

Sub DisplayOldCarColor

Dim strCarColor
strCarColor = "blue"
MsgBox "My old car was" & strCarColor

End Sub

```
Function ReturnNewCarColor

    Dim strCarColor
    strCarColor = "black"
    ReturnNewCarColor = strCarColor

End Function
```

Figure 2.3

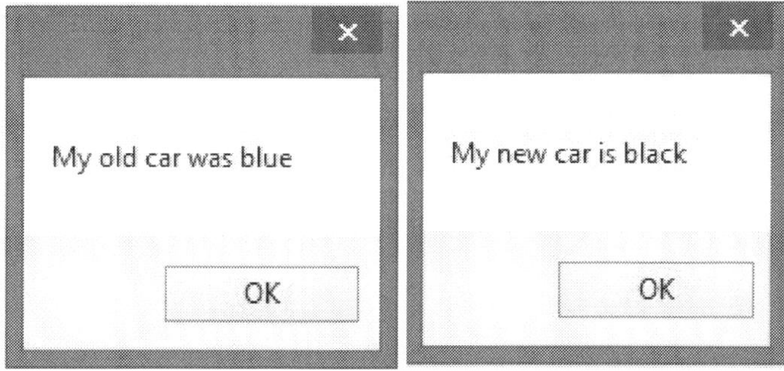

The first output displays “My old car was blue,” using local variable “strCarColor,” while second output displays “My new car is black,” using a local variable “strCarColor” with the same name.

Global variables are variables declared outside of a procedure. All procedures can access global variables. As a result, they cannot have duplicate names. The lifetime of these variables begins when they are declared and ends when the program is closed. Variable lifetime and scope are interrelated. The following are three types/levels of variable scope:

1. Script Level Scope

2. Procedure Level Scope
3. Class Level Scope

Script Level Scope

Script Level Scope (interrelated with global variable) is when the variable is available to all of the scripts in a script file. These variables are not declared in a procedure or class. The following is an example of a variable with script level scope:

Figure 2.4

```
Option Explicit

Dim strFirstName

strFirstName = "Rex"

Call DisplayFirstName(strFirstName)
Call Greet(strFirstName)


Sub DisplayFirstName(strFirst)
    MsgBox "My first name is " & strFirst
End Sub

Sub Greet(strFirst)
    MsgBox "Hello " & strFirst
End Sub
```

Option Explicit

Dim strFirstName

strFirstName = "Rex"

Call DisplayFirstName(strFirstName)

```
Call Greet(strFirstName)

Sub DisplayFirstName(strFirst)
   MsgBox "My first name is " & strFirst
End Sub

Sub Greet(strFirst)
   MsgBox "Hello " & strFirst
End Sub
```

The first output displays “My first name is Rex” using the global variable “strFirstName,” while second output displays “Hello Rex” using the global variable “strFirstName.” Both procedures (DisplayFirstName and Greet) have access to the global variable because the variable has Script Level Scope (available to the entire file).

Figure 2.5

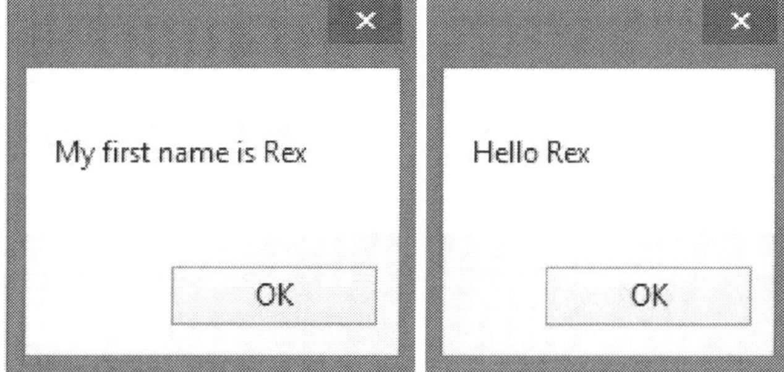

Procedure Level Scope

Procedure Level Scope (interrelated with local variable) is a variable declared in a procedure. Code outside of the procedure does not have access to the variable. The following is an example of a variable with Procedure Level Scope:

Figure 2.6

```
Option Explicit

Call WroteQTP

Sub WroteQTP

    Dim strCompany
    strCompany = "Mercury Interactive"

    MsgBox "Originally, " & strCompany &  " wrote QuickTest Professional"

End Sub
```

Option Explicit

Call WroteQTP

Sub WroteQTP

Dim strCompany
strCompany = "Mercury Interactive"

MsgBox "Originally," & strCompany & "wrote QuickTest Professional"

End Sub

The output displays “Originally, Mercury Interactive wrote QuickTest Professional” by using variable “strCompany” which has procedure level scope.

Skype: rex.jones34
Twitter: @RexJonesII
Email: Rex.Jones@Test4Success.org
LinkedIn: https://www.linkedin.com/in/rexjones34

Figure 2.7

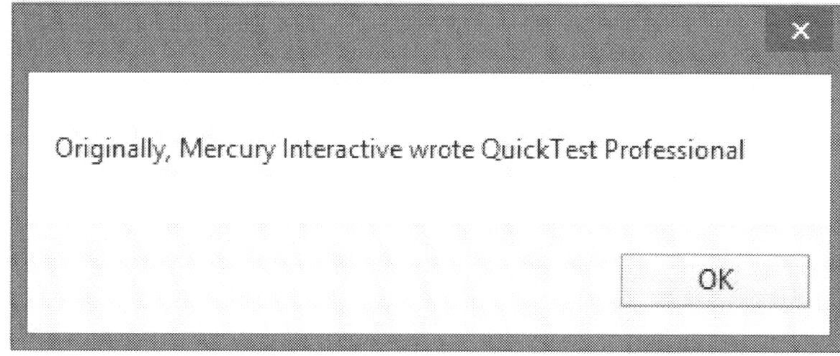

Class Level Scope

Class is a special construct containing logic grouping or properties and methods. Variables declared using the private statement in a class and outside of a procedure within the class has Class Level Scope. Code within the class can access the variable, but code outside of the class cannot access the variable. Variables with Class Level Scope are similar to variables with Procedure Level Scope. The following is an example of a variable "mstrAnimal" with Class Level Scope:

Figure 2.8

```
Option Explicit

Class Animals

        Private mstrAnimal

        Public Property Let Zebra (strAnimal)
                mstrAnimal = strAnimal
        End Property

        Public Sub ZebraColor (strColor)
                MsgBox mstrAnimal & " look good with a " & DisplayCarColor (strColor) & " color."
        End Sub

        Private Function DisplayCarColor (strColor)
                Select Case strColor
                        Case "Black and White"
                                DisplayCarColor = "Black and White"
                        Case "Brown and White"
                                DisplayCarColor = "Brown and White"
                        Case "Brown and Black"
                                DisplayCarColor = "Brown and Black"
                End Select
        End Function

End Class
```

Option Explicit

Class Animals

Private mstrAnimal

Public Property Let Zebra (strAnimal)
mstrAnimal = strAnimal
End Property

Public Sub ZebraColor (strColor)
MsgBox mstrAnimal & " look good with a " & DisplayCarColor (strColor) & "color."

```
    End Sub

    Private Function DisplayCarColor (strColor)
        Select Case strColor
            Case "Black and White"
                DisplayCarColor = "Black and White"
            Case "Brown and White"
                DisplayCarColor = "Brown and White"
            Case "Brown and Black"
                DisplayCarColor = "Brown and Black"
        End Select
    End Function

End Class
```

Declare Variables

We can declare variables with Dim, Public, or Private Statements. All variables are available regardless of the statement type. The three statements are listed below:

1. Dim Statement
2. Public Statement
3. Private Statement

Dim Statement

The Dim statement permits one or more new variables to be declared while allocating memory. This statement is used to declare variables at the Script Level or Procedure Level. Public and Private Statements are not allowed inside of a Procedure Level. Dim Statements are similar to a Public Statement, if used within the Class Level.

```
Dim strTestPage
```

Public Statement

The Public statement permits one or more new variables and/or arrays to be declared while allocating memory. This statement is used at the Script Level or Class Level, but not in a procedure. It is recommended to use a Public Statement within a Class. The following is the syntax for a Public Statement:

Public strTestPage

Private Statement

The Private statement permits one or more new variables and/or arrays to be declared while allocating memory. This statement is used at the Script Level or Class Level, but not in a procedure. If a Private Statement is declared outside of a procedure, then the results have the same effect as a Dim Statement or a Public Statement. Variables outside of a procedure are available to the entire script file (known as a global variable). This forces the Private Statement to operate like a Dim or Public Statement. The following is the syntax for a Private Statement:

Private strTestPage

More than one variable declaration is allowed on the same line. However, there are limitations on the number of variables within a script and procedure. 127 variables is the maximum for Script and Procedure Level variables. The following is an example of multiple variable declarations on one line and using multiple statements to declare variables:

Multiple Variables on One Line

Dim strTestPage, strFirstName, strLastName

Multiple Statements Using Public and Private Statements

Public strTestPage, strUserName, strPassCode
Private strFirstName, strLastName

Option Explicit

VBScript is a loosely-typed language, which does not require programmers to declare the data type of a variable. Programming languages are classified as loosely-typed when the data type can hold any kind of data. Therefore, variables are not required to be explicitly declared. However, this convenience can be risky to utilize. Variables can be misspelled when automatically declared, which is a problem that VBScript will not catch. VBScript assumes that the Programmer is creating a new variable, then allocates memory and provides an “Empty” Sub-Data Type.

The accident of misspelling variables can be prevented by using an “Option Explicit” Statement. Option Explicit is placed at the top of each script file and applies to the entire script file. This informs VBScript that all variables should be explicitly declared before they can be used. When Option Explicit is implemented in the file, then an error occurs when there is a typing error with a variable. The following is an example of an Option Explicit Statement:

Figure 2.9

```
Option Explicit

Dim strMessage

strMessage = "Option Explicit is very important in VBScript"
MsgBox strMessage
```

Option Explicit

Dim strMessage

strMessage = "Option Explicit is very important in VBScript"
MsgBox strMessage

3 Tips To Master QTP/UFT Within 30 Days
http://tinyurl.com/3-Tips-For-QTP-UFT

Free Webinars, Videos, and Live Trainings
http://tinyurl.com/Free-QTP-UFT-Selenium

The output displays "Option Explicit is very important in VBScript"

Figure 2.10

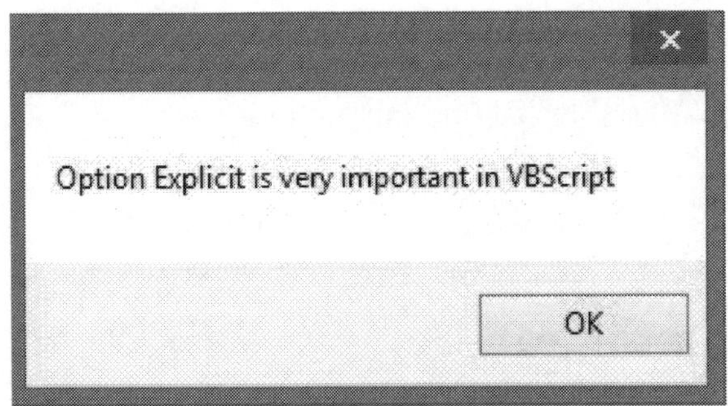

Data Types

All variables have a variant data type. Variant is a special data type that contains different kinds of information according to how it is used. The information will be in numeric or string form. There are distinctions with numeric information ranging in size from Boolean Values to Floating Point Numbers. Several categories of string and numeric Variant information are called Sub-Data Types. The following are Sub-Data Types:

Figure 2.11

Sub-Data Type	Description
Empty	Value is "0" or an empty value. The variable is uninitialized when it is created and no value is assigned to it when the variable is set to empty
Null	Variable with invalid data
Boolean	Contains either True or False
Byte	Contains numeric values ranging from 0 to 255
Integer	Contains numeric values ranging from -32,768 to 32,767
Currency	Contains a currency value ranging from -922,337,203,685,477.5808 to 922,337,203,685, 477.5807

Long	Contains numeric values ranging from -2,147,483,648 to 2,147,483,647
Single	Contains a single-precision, floating-point number
Double	Contains a double-precision, floating-point number
Date (Time)	Contains a date and time
String	Contains alphanumeric character(s) stored in double quotes
Object	Contains an object
Error	Contains an error number

Hungarian Naming Convention

The Hungarian Naming Convention involves giving variable names to a prefix. As a result, the prefix indicates the variable's data type and scope. The Hungarian Naming Convention makes programs easier to write and read. It is best to use the "var" prefix if the Programmer is unsure what type of data might end up in the variable or if the Programmer is intending to use different kinds of data at different times.

Figure 2.12

Data Type	Prefix	Example
Boolean	bln or bool	blnBusy
Byte	byt	bytColor
Currency	cur	curDollar
Date or Time	dtm	dtmToday
Double	dbl	dblAmount
Error	err	errInvalid
Integer	int	intTotal
Long	lng	lngWeight
Object	obj	objSchedule
Single	sng	sngMeasure
String	str	strTest
Variant	var	varTeam

3 Tips To Master QTP/UFT Within 30 Days
http://tinyurl.com/3-Tips-For-QTP-UFT

Free Webinars, Videos, and Live Trainings
http://tinyurl.com/Free-QTP-UFT-Selenium

Chapter 2 mentioned the variable rules, variable types, and variable lifetime. In addition, the data types, Option Explicit, Variable declaration, and naming convention for variables were explained. Chapter 3 focuses on Operators and their precedence.

Skype: rex.jones34
Twitter: @RexJonesII
Email: Rex.Jones@Test4Success.org
LinkedIn: https://www.linkedin.com/in/rexjones34

Chapter 3
Operators

Operators are symbols that represent a specific action. They allow programmers to manipulate numbers and text by performing a function on one or more inputs. The following are the different types of operators:

- **Assignment Operator**: Used for assigning a value to a property or a variable
- **Arithmetic Operator**: Used to calculate a numeric value and used with the assignment operator and/or comparison operator
- **Concatenation Operator**: Used to join an infinite number of expressions together. The Concatenation Operator is considered a stand-alone operator type, but is sometimes included with the Arithmetic Operator
- **Comparison Operator**: Used for comparing variables and expressions
- **Logical Operator**: Used for performing logical operations on expressions. A logical operation is an operation that is used to control the flow of a program. All logical operators can be used as Bitwise Operators
- **Bitwise Operator**: Used for computing binary values bit by bit (All bitwise operators can be used as logical operators)

Operations are normally performed from left to right, unless there is more than one operator in an expression. If more than one operator exists within an expression, then they are executed in the following order: Arithmetic Operators are executed first, followed by the Concatenation Operator, then Comparison Operators, and finally Logical Operators.

The order can be overridden by using parentheses. Operations that are placed in parentheses are always evaluated before operations outside of the parentheses. Normal precedent rules apply within the parentheses. The following are a couple of examples:

y = 3 + 2 * 4 + 5
y = (3 + 2) * (4 + 5)

```
Option Explicit
Dim y

y = 3 + 2 * 4 + 5
MsgBox y
```

The answer is 16.

Figure 3.1

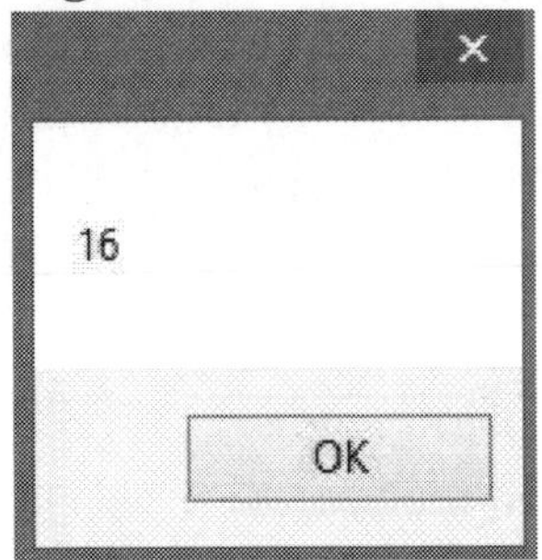


```
Option Explicit
Dim y

y = (3 + 2) * (4 + 5)
MsgBox y
```

The answer is 45.

Figure 3.2

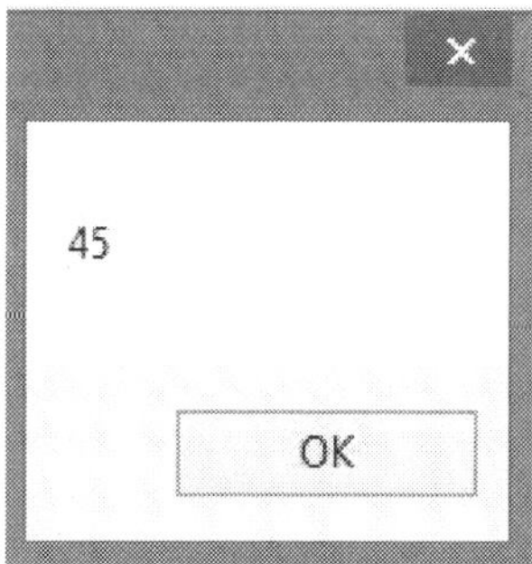

The two examples above look similar, but are actually different. According to the guidelines of operator precedence, multiplication is evaluated prior to addition. Therefore, the first line has a value of 16 (2 * 4 = 8 + 3 + 5 = 16). By adding parentheses, the addition operators are evaluated before the multiplication operators, therefore the second line has a value of 45 (5 * 9 = 45).

This chapter will cover four of the Operator Types. The Concatenation Operator is included within the Arithmetic Operator. The operators which will be discussed are as follows:

- ✓ Arithmetic Operators
- ✓ Comparison Operators
- ✓ Logical Operators

Arithmetic Operators

An Arithmetic Operator is a function that takes operands and uses them to perform a calculation or to join an expression. For example, the following expression: 7 = 3 + 4 uses the Addition Operator (+) to add two operands: 3 and 4. Arithmetic Operators are combined with the Assignment Operator and/or one of the Comparison Operators. The following is a list of each of the Arithmetic Operators in order of precedence:

3 Tips To Master QTP/UFT Within 30 Days
http://tinyurl.com/3-Tips-For-QTP-UFT

Free Webinars, Videos, and Live Trainings
http://tinyurl.com/Free-QTP-UFT-Selenium

- Exponentiation
- Unary Negation
- Multiplication
- Floating Point Division
- Integer Division
- Modulus Arithmetic
- Addition
- Subtraction
- Concatenation

Exponentiation

The Exponentiation Operator (^) is used to raise a number to the power of an exponent. The following is an example of an Exponentiation Operator:

Syntax
Result = Number ^ Exponent

```
Option Explicit
Dim x, y

x = 7
y = x ^ 2
MsgBox y
```

The answer is 49.

Skype: rex.jones34
Twitter: @RexJonesII
Email: Rex.Jones@Test4Success.org
LinkedIn: https://www.linkedin.com/in/rexjones34

Figure 3.3

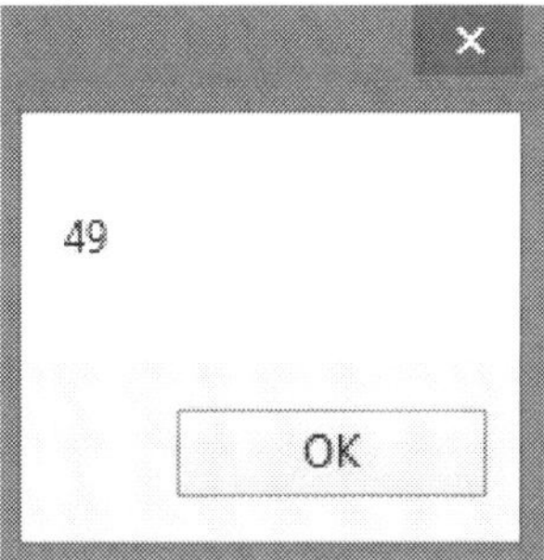

Note: Numbers can be negative if the exponent is an integer. The exponent is evaluated from left to right, if more than one exponent is in a single expression. The result is always "Null" if the number or exponent is Null.

Unary Negation

The Unary Negation Operator (-) indicates the negative value of a numeric expression. It only applies to one value or variable. The following is an example of the Unary Negation Operator:

Syntax
- Number

```
Option Explicit
Dim x

x = -45
MsgBox x
```

The answer represents a negative number "-45".

3 Tips To Master QTP/UFT Within 30 Days
http://tinyurl.com/3-Tips-For-QTP-UFT

Free Webinars, Videos, and Live Trainings
http://tinyurl.com/Free-QTP-UFT-Selenium

Figure 3.4

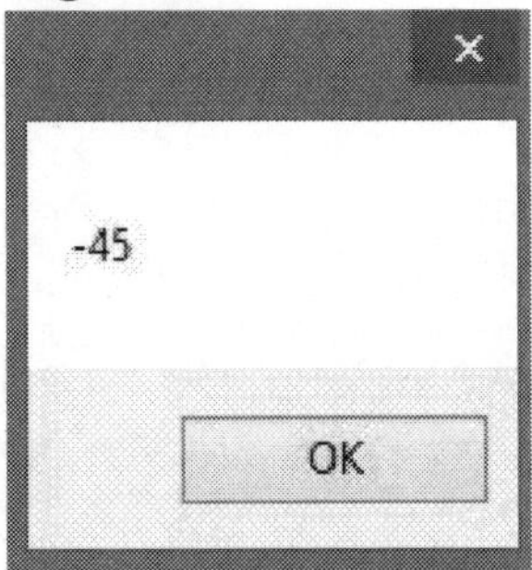

Note: Empty expressions are treated as a zero (0). The result is Null if one or both expressions are Null.

Multiplication

The Multiplication Operator (*) is used to multiply two numbers. The following is an example of the Multiplication Operator:

Syntax
Result = Number1 * Number2

```
Option Explicit
Dim x
x = 3 * 4
MsgBox x
```

The answer is 12.

Skype: rex.jones34
Twitter: @RexJonesII
Email: Rex.Jones@Test4Success.org
LinkedIn: https://www.linkedin.com/in/rexjones34

Figure 3.5

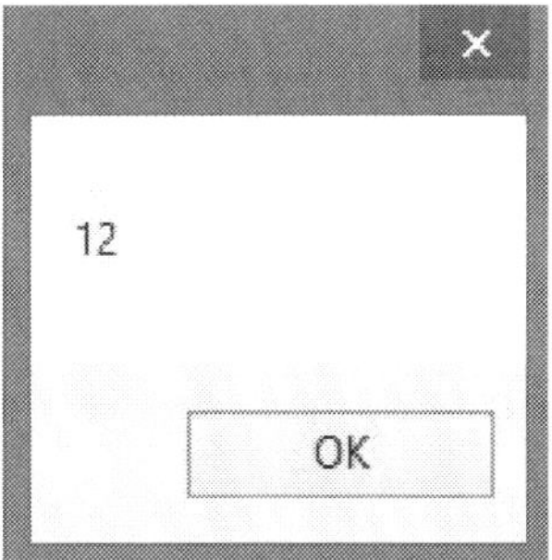

Note: Empty expressions are treated as a zero (0). The result is Null if one or both expressions are Null.

Floating Point Division

The Floating Point Division Operator (/) is used to divide two numbers and return a floating point number. A floating point number is when there are no fixed numbers of digits before and after the decimal point. The following is an example of the Floating Point Division Operator:

Syntax
Result = Number1 / Number2

```
Option Explicit
Dim x

x = 4 / 3
MsgBox x
```

The answer is 1.33333333333333

3 Tips To Master QTP/UFT Within 30 Days
http://tinyurl.com/3-Tips-For-QTP-UFT

Free Webinars, Videos, and Live Trainings
http://tinyurl.com/Free-QTP-UFT-Selenium

Figure 3.6

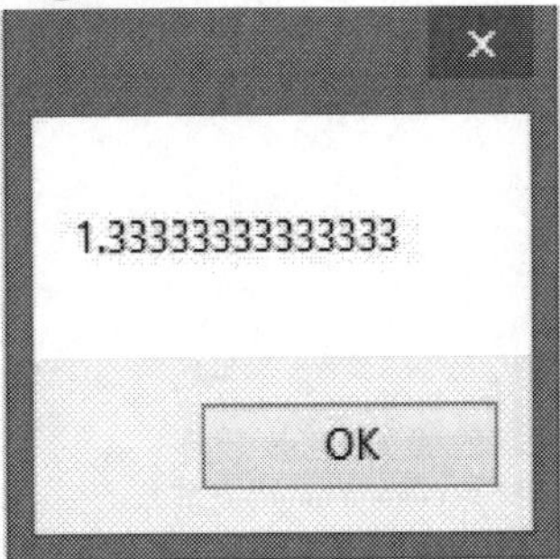

Note: Empty expressions are treated as a zero (0). The result is Null if one or both expressions are Null.

Integer Division

The Integer Division Operator (\) is used to divide two numbers, discard the remainder, and return only the integer. The following is an example of the Integer Division Operator:

Syntax
Result = Number1 \ Number2

```
Option Explicit
Dim x

x = 4 \ 3
MsgBox x
```

The answer is 1.

Skype: rex.jones34
Twitter: @RexJonesII
Email: Rex.Jones@Test4Success.org
LinkedIn: https://www.linkedin.com/in/rexjones34

Figure 3.7

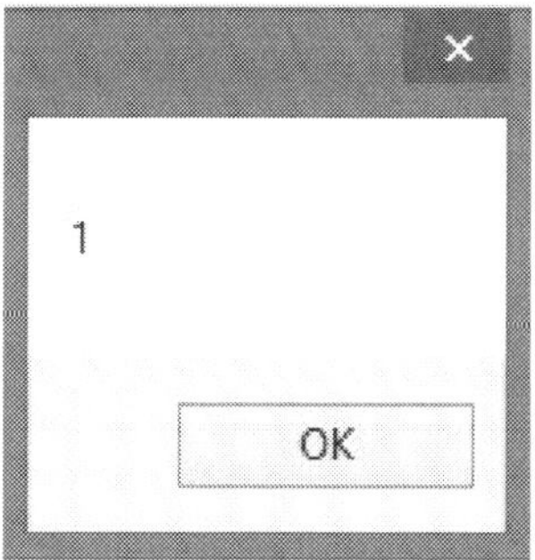

Note: Empty expressions are treated as a zero (0). The result is Null if one or both expressions are Null.

Modulus Arithmetic

The Modulus Arithmetic Operator (Mod) is used to divide two numbers and return only the remainder. The following is an example of the Modulus Arithmetic Operator:

Syntax
Result = Number1 Mod Number2

```
Option Explicit
Dim x

x = 12 Mod 10
MsgBox x
```

The answer is 2.

Figure 3.8

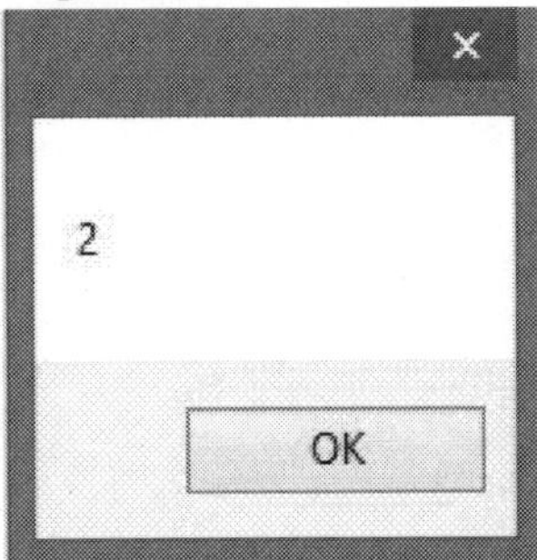

Note: Numbers are rounded to integers if they are floating point numbers. Empty expressions are treated as a zero (0). The result is Null if one or both expressions are Null.

Addition

The Addition Operator (+) is used to add numbers and join strings. The following is an example of the Addition Operator:

Syntax
Result = Number1 + Number2

```
Option Explicit
Dim x

x = 3 + 4
MsgBox x
```

The answer is 7.

Skype: rex.jones34
Twitter: @RexJonesII
Email: Rex.Jones@Test4Success.org
LinkedIn: https://www.linkedin.com/in/rexjones34

Figure 3.9

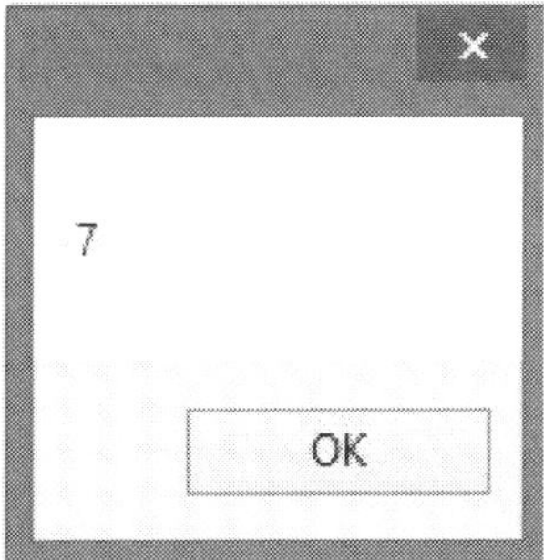

Note: The result is an integer if both expressions are Empty. However, if one expression is Empty, then the other expression is unchanged. The result is Null if one or both expressions are Null. Expressions determine the Addition Operator's (+) behavior. If strings are involved, then the Addition Operator will combine the strings like the Concatenation Operator (&). The following is an example of the Addition Operator combining strings together:

```
Option Explicit

Dim strFirstName, strLastName

strFirstName = "John"
strLastName = "Doe"

MsgBox "A common fake name is " + strFirstName + " " + strLastName
```

The output displays "A common fake name is John Doe."

3 Tips To Master QTP/UFT Within 30 Days
http://tinyurl.com/3-Tips-For-QTP-UFT

Free Webinars, Videos, and Live Trainings
http://tinyurl.com/Free-QTP-UFT-Selenium

Figure 3.10

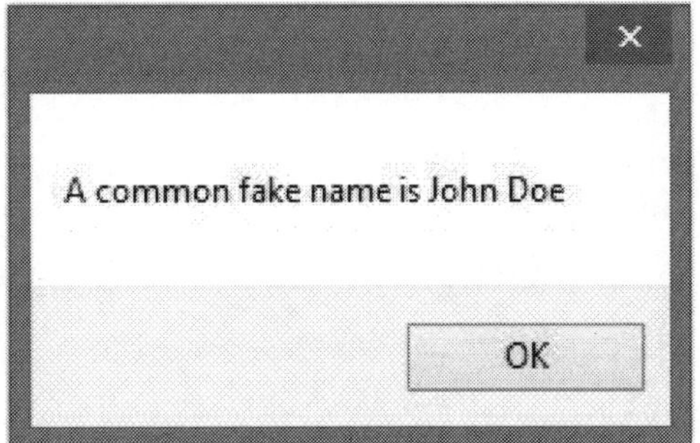

The following is a Success Table that shows different types of expressions:

Figure 3.11

If	Then
Both expressions are numeric	Add
Both expressions are strings	Concatenate
One expression is numeric and the other is a string	Error: Type Mismatch

Subtraction

The Subtraction Operator (-) is used to find the difference between two numbers. The following is an example of the Subtraction Operator:

Syntax
Result = Number1 – Number2

```
Option Explicit
Dim x

x = 37 - 3
```

Skype: rex.jones34
Twitter: @RexJonesII
Email: Rex.Jones@Test4Success.org
LinkedIn: https://www.linkedin.com/in/rexjones34

MsgBox x

The answer is 34.

Figure 3.12

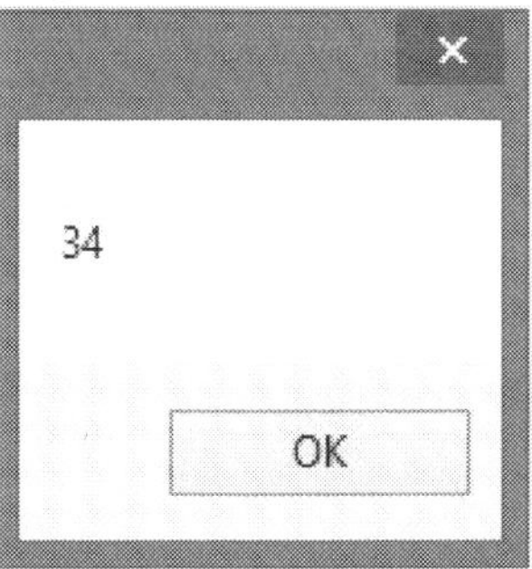

Note: Empty expressions are treated as a zero (0). The result is Null if one or both expressions are Null.

Concatenation

The Concatenation Operator (&) is used to force a concatenation of expressions. The following is an example of the Concatenation Operator:

Syntax
Result = Expression1 & Expression2

Option Explicit

Dim strFirstName, strLastName

strFirstName = "Rex"
strLastName = "Jones II"

MsgBox "The author of this eBook is " & strFirstName & " " & strLastName & "."

The answer is “The author of this eBook is Rex Jones II.”

Figure 3.13

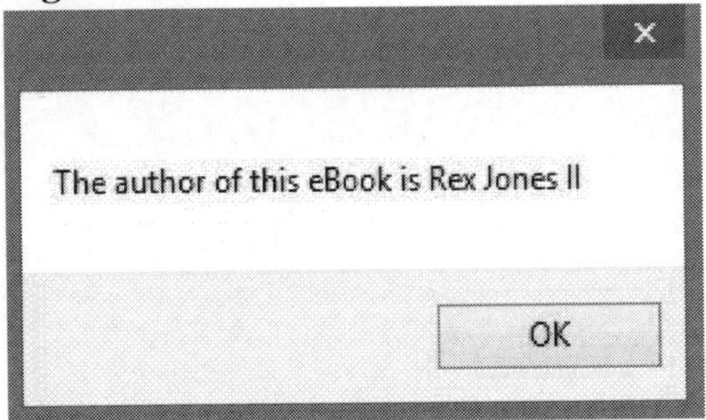

Note: Non-String expressions are converted to strings. If both expressions are Null, then the result is also Null. However, if only one expression is Null, then that expression is treated as a zero-length string (" ") when concatenated with the other expression. A zero-length string is given a blank value—no value. Any expression that is Empty is also treated as a zero-length string.

Comparison Operators

Comparison operators allow the programmer to compare two expressions. Comparison Operators test whether two expressions are True or False. Therefore, the data type of a Comparison Operator is Boolean.

The following is a Success Table, which is a guideline for comparing expressions:

Figure 3.14

If	Then

Both expressions are numeric	Perform a numeric comparison
Both expressions are strings	Perform a string comparison
One expression is numeric and the other is a string	The numeric expression is less than the string expression
One expression is Empty and the other is numeric	Perform a numeric comparison, using zero (0) as the Empty expression
One expression is Empty and the other is a string	Perform a string comparison, using a zero-length string ("") as the Empty expression
Both expressions are Empty	The expressions are equal

The following is a list of each Comparison Operator in order of precedence:

- Equality
- Inequality
- Less Than
- Greater Than
- Less Than or Equal To
- Greater Than or Equal To
- Object Equivalence (Is)

Equality

The Equality Operator (=) returns True if Expression1 equals Expression2, and returns False otherwise. The following is an example of the Equality Operator:

3 Tips To Master QTP/UFT Within 30 Days
http://tinyurl.com/3-Tips-For-QTP-UFT

Free Webinars, Videos, and Live Trainings
http://tinyurl.com/Free-QTP-UFT-Selenium

Syntax
Expression1 = Expression2

Option Explicit
Dim x, y

x = 34
y = 34

If x = y **Then**
 MsgBox x & "equals " & y
End If

The expression is a true statement that displays 34 equals 34.

Figure 3.15

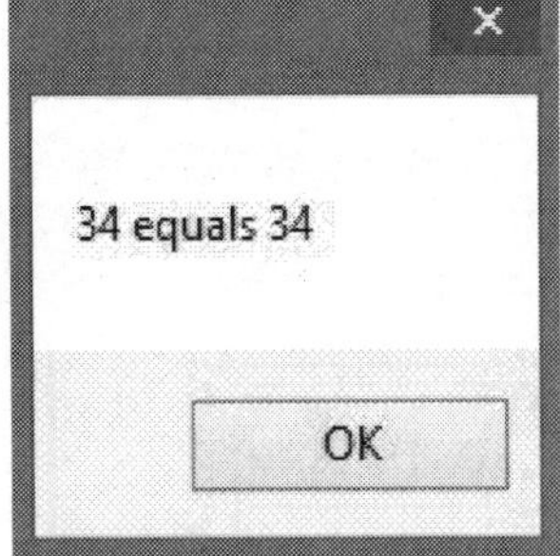

Inequality

The Inequality Operator (<>) returns True if Expression1 does not equal Expression2, and returns False otherwise. The following is an example of the Inequality Operator:

Syntax
Expression1 <> Expression2

```
Option Explicit
Dim x, y

x = 34
y = 38

If x <> y Then
   MsgBox x & "does not equal" & y
End If
```

The expression is a true statement that displays 34 does not equal 38.

Figure 3.16

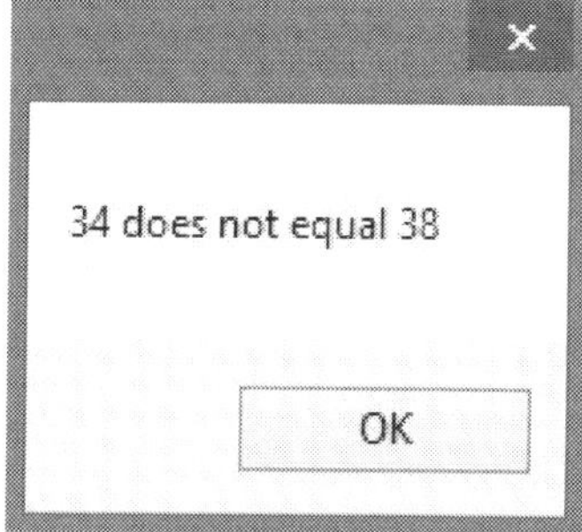

Less Than

The Less Than Operator (<) returns True if Expression1 is less than Expression2, and returns False otherwise. The following is an example of the Less Than Operator:

Syntax

Expression1 < Expression2

```
Option Explicit
Dim x, y
```

```
x = 34
y = 38

If x < y Then
   MsgBox x & "is less than" & y
End If
```

The expression is a true statement that displays 34 is less than 38.

Figure 3.17

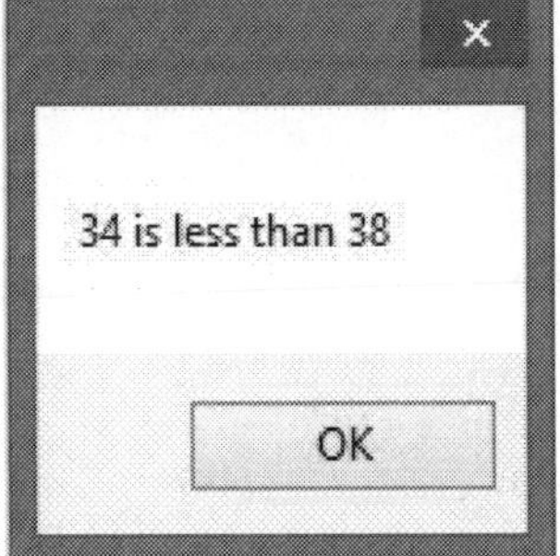

Greater Than

The Greater Than Operator (>) returns True if Expression1 is greater than Expression2, and returns False otherwise. The following is an example of the Greater Than Operator:

Syntax
Expression1 > Expression2

```
Option Explicit
Dim x, y

x = 38
y = 34
```

Skype: rex.jones34
Twitter: @RexJonesII
Email: Rex.Jones@Test4Success.org
LinkedIn: https://www.linkedin.com/in/rexjones34

```
If x > y Then
   MsgBox x & "is greater than" & y
End If
```

The expression is a true statement that displays 38 is greater than 34.

Figure 3.18

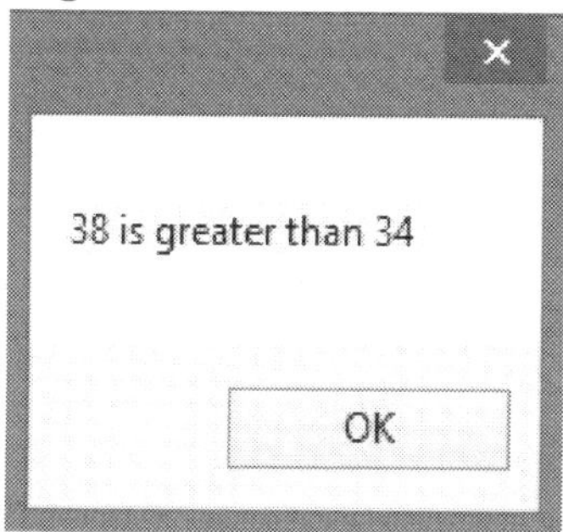

Less Than or Equal To

The Less Than or Equal To Operator (<=) returns True if Expression1 is less than or equal to Expression2, and returns False otherwise. The following is an example of the Less Than or Equal To Operator:

Syntax
Expression1 <= Expression2

```
Option Explicit
Dim x, y

x = 34
y = 34
```

```
If x <= y Then
   MsgBox x & "is less than or equal to" & y
End If
```

The expression is a true statement that displays 34 is less than or equal to 34.

Figure 3.19

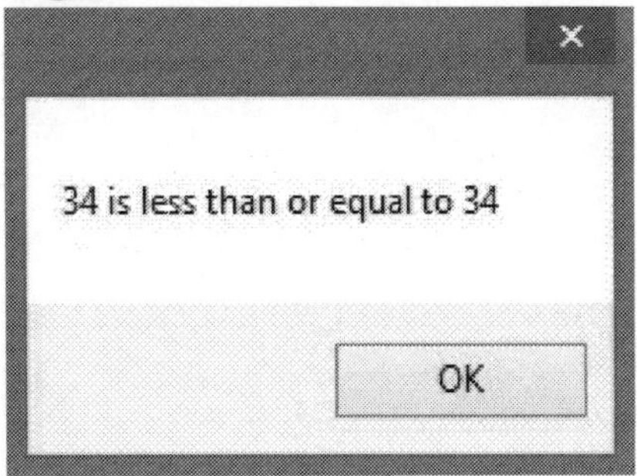


```
Option Explicit
Dim x, y

x = 34
y = 38

If x <= y Then
   MsgBox x & "is less than or equal to" & y
End If
```

The expression is a true statement that displays 34 is less than or equal to 38.

Skype: rex.jones34
Twitter: @RexJonesII
Email: Rex.Jones@Test4Success.org
LinkedIn: https://www.linkedin.com/in/rexjones34

Figure 3.20

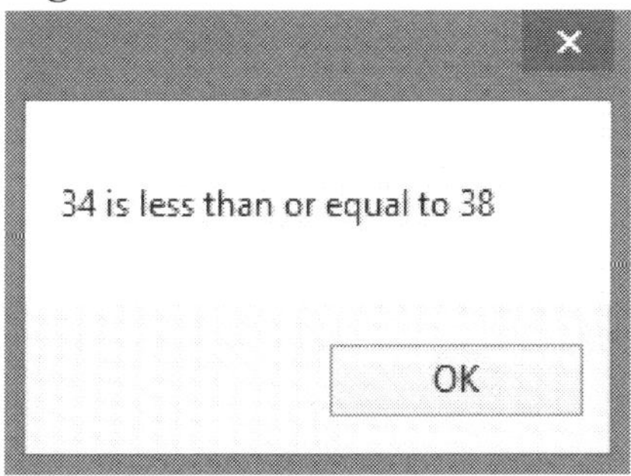

Greater Than or Equal To

The Greater Than or Equal To Operator (>=) returns True if Expression1 is greater than or equal to Expression2, and returns False otherwise. The following is an example of the Greater Than or Equal To Operator:

Syntax
Expression1 >= Expression2

```
Option Explicit
Dim x, y

x = 34
y = 34

If x >= y Then
   MsgBox x & "is greater than or equal to" & y
End If
```

The expression is a true statement that displays 34 is greater than or equal to 34.

3 Tips To Master QTP/UFT Within 30 Days
http://tinyurl.com/3-Tips-For-QTP-UFT

Free Webinars, Videos, and Live Trainings
http://tinyurl.com/Free-QTP-UFT-Selenium

Figure 3.21

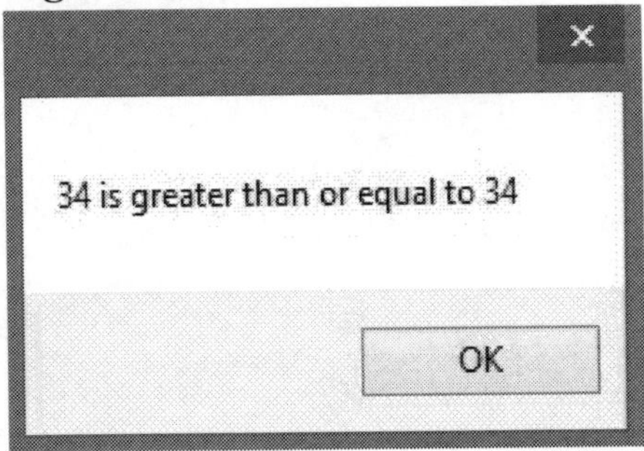


```
Option Explicit
Dim x, y

x = 38
y = 34

If x >= y Then
   MsgBox x & "is greater than or equal to" & y
End If
```

The output displays “38 is greater than or equal to 34”

Skype: rex.jones34
Twitter: @RexJonesII
Email: Rex.Jones@Test4Success.org
LinkedIn: https://www.linkedin.com/in/rexjones34

Figure 3.22

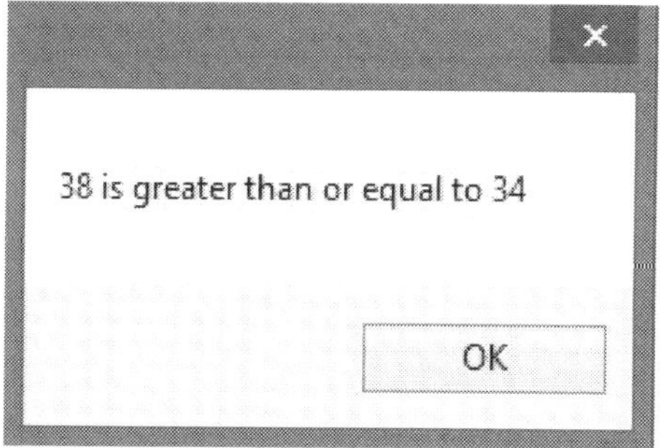

Object Equivalence (Is)

The Object Equivalence (Is) returns True, if Object1 and Object2 refer to the same memory location. The following is an example of the Object Equivalence Operator (Is):

Syntax
Result = Object1 Is Object2

```
Option Explicit
Dim x, y, z
Dim intSameNumber

x = 11
y = 21
z = "1 on another level"

Set x = CreateObject("Scripting.Dictionary")
Set y = CreateObject("Scripting.Dictionary")
Set z = CreateObject("Scripting.Dictionary")

Set x = z
```

3 Tips To Master QTP/UFT Within 30 Days
http://tinyurl.com/3-Tips-For-QTP-UFT

Free Webinars, Videos, and Live Trainings
http://tinyurl.com/Free-QTP-UFT-Selenium

Set y = z

intSameNumber = x **Is** y
MsgBox intSameNumber

The answer is "True."

Figure 3.23

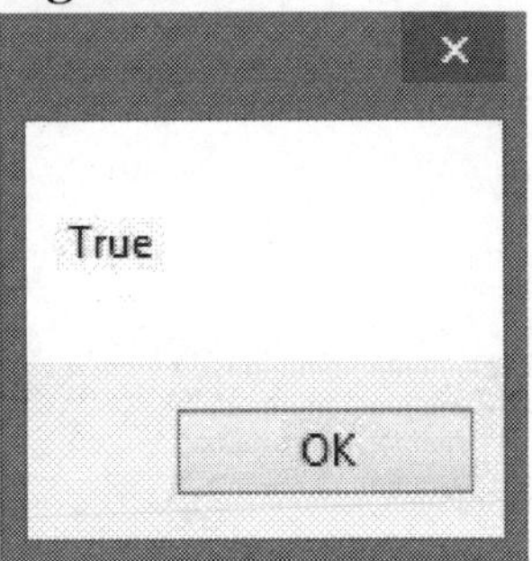

Note: Object Equivalence Operator (Is) does not compare values or compare one object to another object. Instead, it checks if two objects (x and y) in the same expression refer to the same object (z), which is the same memory location.

Logical Operators

The Logical Operators are used for performing logical operations on expressions. It is customary to find logical operators in control statements to control the program's flow. Each operand is considered a decision, which allows the program to make a decision. The following are types of each Logical Operators in order of precedence:

- Logical Negation (Not)
- Logical Conjunction (And)
- Logical Disjunction (Or)
- Logical Exclusion (Xor)

- Logical Equivalence (Eqv)
- Logical Implication (Imp)

Logical Negation (Not)

The Logical Negation Operator (Not) returns the logical negation of an expression. The results will be True if the expression is False and False if the expression is True. Null will be returned if the expression is Null. The following is an example of the Logical Negation Operator:

Syntax
Result = Not Expression

Option Explicit
Dim x, y

x = 10
y = **Not (x < 20)**
MsgBox y

The answer is "False."

Figure 3.24

3 Tips To Master QTP/UFT Within 30 Days
http://tinyurl.com/3-Tips-For-QTP-UFT

Free Webinars, Videos, and Live Trainings
http://tinyurl.com/Free-QTP-UFT-Selenium

The following is a Success Table for the Logical Negation Operator (Not):

Figure 3.25

Expression	Result
True	False
False	True
Null	Null

Logical Conjunction (And)

The Logical Conjunction Operator (And) returns True if both expressions are True, and returns False otherwise. The following is an example of the Logical Conjunction Operator:

Syntax
Result = Expression1 And Expression2

```
Option Explicit
Dim x, y, z

x = 10
y = 15

z = x > 4 And y <=20
MsgBox z
```

The answer is "True."

Skype: rex.jones34
Twitter: @RexJonesII
Email: Rex.Jones@Test4Success.org
LinkedIn: https://www.linkedin.com/in/rexjones34

Figure 3.26

The following is a Success Table for the Logical Conjunction Operator (And):

Figure 3.27

If Expression1	**If Expression2**	**Expression1 And Expression2**
True	True	True
True	False	False
False	True	False
False	False	False

Logical Disjunction (Or)

The Logical Disjunction Operator (Or) returns True if one or both expressions are True, and returns False otherwise. The following is an example of the Logical Disjunction Operator:

Syntax
Result = Expression1 Or Expression2

```
Option Explicit
Dim x, y, z

x = 10
```

3 Tips To Master QTP/UFT Within 30 Days
http://tinyurl.com/3-Tips-For-QTP-UFT

Free Webinars, Videos, and Live Trainings
http://tinyurl.com/Free-QTP-UFT-Selenium

y = 15
z = x > 4 **Or** y >=20
MsgBox z

The answer is "True."

Figure 3.28

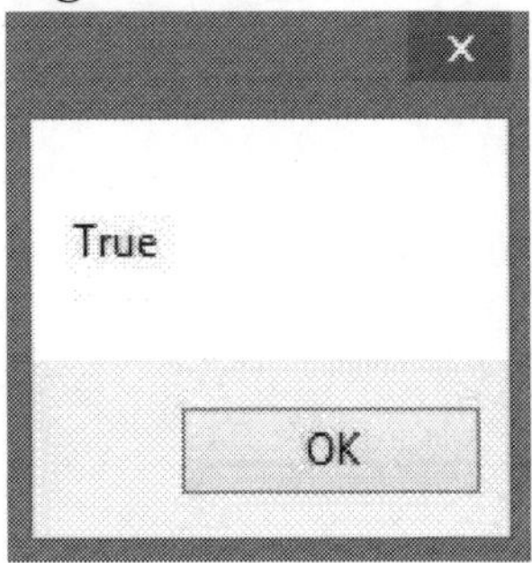

The following is a Success Table for the Logical Disjunction Operator (Or):

Figure 3.29

If Expression1	If Expression2	Expression1 Or Expression2
True	True	True
True	False	True
False	True	True
False	False	False

Logical Exclusion (Xor)

The Logical Exclusion Operator (Xor) returns True if only one expression is True, and otherwise returns False. The following is an example of the Logical Exclusion Operator:

Syntax
Result = Expression1 Xor Expression2

```
Option Explicit
Dim x, y, z

x = 100
y = 10
z = x = 200 Xor y > 400
MsgBox z
```

The answer is "False."

Figure 3.30

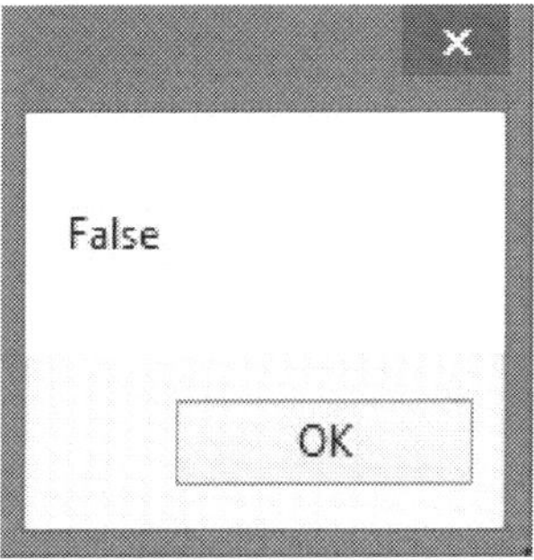

The following is a Success Table for the Logical Exclusion Operator (Xor):

Figure 3.31

If Expression1	If Expression2	Expression1 Xor Expression2
True	True	False
True	False	True

3 Tips To Master QTP/UFT Within 30 Days
http://tinyurl.com/3-Tips-For-QTP-UFT

Free Webinars, Videos, and Live Trainings
http://tinyurl.com/Free-QTP-UFT-Selenium

False	True	True
False	False	False

Logical Equivalence (Eqv)

The Logical Equivalence Operator (Eqv) returns True, if both expressions evaluate to the same value (True or False). The following is an example of the Logical Equivalence Operator:

Syntax
Result = Expression1 Eqv Expression2

```
Option Explicit
Dim x, y, z

x = 100
y = 10
z = x > 200 Eqv y > 400
MsgBox z
```

The answer is "True."

Figure 3.32

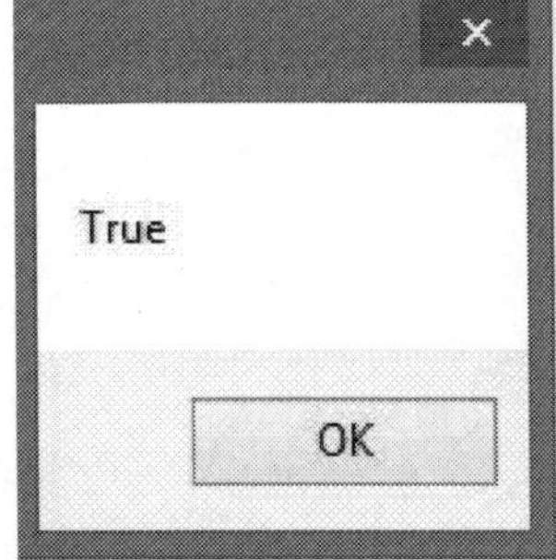

Skype: rex.jones34
Twitter: @RexJonesII
Email: Rex.Jones@Test4Success.org
LinkedIn: https://www.linkedin.com/in/rexjones34

The following is a Success Table for the Logical Equivalence Operator (Eqv):

Figure 3.33

If Expression1	If Expression2	Expression1 Eqv Expression2
True	True	True
True	False	False
False	True	False
False	False	True

Logical Implication (Imp)

The Logical Implication Operator (Imp) only returns False, if Expression1 is True and Expression2 is False. The following is an example of the Logical Implication Operator:

Syntax
Result = Expression1 Imp Expression2

```
---------------------------------------

Option Explicit
Dim x, y, z

x = 45
y = 50
z = x < 200 Imp y > 40
MsgBox z
```

The answer is "True."

3 Tips To Master QTP/UFT Within 30 Days
http://tinyurl.com/3-Tips-For-QTP-UFT

Free Webinars, Videos, and Live Trainings
http://tinyurl.com/Free-QTP-UFT-Selenium

Figure 3.34

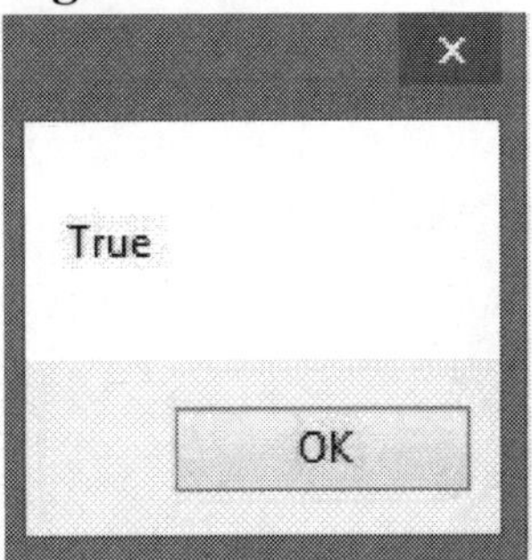

The following is a Success Table for the Logical Implication Operator (Imp):

Figure 3.35

If Expression1	**If Expression2**	**Expression1 Imp Expression2**
True	True	True
True	False	False
False	True	True
False	False	True

Chapter 3 discussed four of the six Operator types: Arithmetic, Concatenation, Comparison, and Logical. Chapter 4 will explain Arrays, which stores values similar to a variable.

Chapter 4 Arrays

An array is a matrix of data that stores multiple values. It is allowed to accommodate multiple pieces of information in multiple compartments. Compartments separate data into divisions or sections for a specific operation. The same concept applies to arrays as variables, except variables can only hold one value. Arrays are declared with a parentheses and Hungarian prefix of "arr" or "a." They can be used to store parameters passed from the test data sheet and to store values from the application.

Chapter four covers:

Declare Array and Bounds

An array can be declared several ways, depending on how it is created. It can be created with values, a Split Function, statically, or dynamically. Coincidentally, the two types of arrays are also Static and Dynamic.

Static Array Type

Static Arrays have a constant index. It is not possible to increase or decrease the array size. The array remains a fixed size throughout the lifetime of its existence. Therefore, programmers must know how many items will be in the array. Arrays can be as simple as a single column or complicated displaying 60 dimensions. Nevertheless, most arrays have one or two dimensions.

3 Tips To Master QTP/UFT Within 30 Days
http://tinyurl.com/3-Tips-For-QTP-UFT

Free Webinars, Videos, and Live Trainings
http://tinyurl.com/Free-QTP-UFT-Selenium

One-Dimensional Array

A One-Dimensional Array has a list of rows and only one column. The number in parenthesis specifies the maximum value of indexes. Index is an integer subscript that denotes an item's relative location in a list. The following is an example of a One-Dimensional Array:

Dim arrName(2)

Fill One-Dimensional Array

New arrays will be empty if an array function is not used. Items must be assigned to indexes for arrays to be filled. The following is an example of a filled One-Dimensional Array:

Figure 4.1

```
arrName(0) = "James"
arrName(1) = "Janice"
arrName(2) = "Jane"
```

arrName(0) = "James"
arrName(1) = "Janice"
arrName(2) = "Jane"

Figure 4.2

NameOfArray(index)	Value	Item #
arrName(0)	James	1
arrName(1)	Janice	2
arrName(2)	Jane	3

The value in parentheses fills a specific index. This example fills zero (0) with "James," one (1) with "Janice," and two (2) with "Jane." Therefore, the array holds three items starting from index 0 and ending with index 2. Zero is the lower bound and two is the upper bound. Arrays are zero-based and always have a zero lower bound. On the other hand, VBScript allows the upper bound to be determined. The upper bound dictates how many compartments a particular dimension can hold. Each of the compartments in an array are called an element. One element can accommodate only one value.

LBound

LBound is a function that returns the smallest subscript for a dimension of an array. The following is an example of the LBound Function:

Syntax
LBound (NameOfArray[, Dimension])

Figure 4.3

Parameter	Description
NameOfArray	Required. An array variable name
Dimension	Optional. Basic dimensions define 1 as a column and 2 as a row. Dimensions may continue past 2. The default dimension is 1

Figure 4.4

```
Option Explicit
Dim arrName(2)

arrName(0) = "James"
arrName(1) = "Janice"
arrName(2) = "Jane"

MsgBox LBound(arrName, 1)
'or
MsgBox LBound(arrName)
```

Option Explicit
Dim arrName(2)

3 Tips To Master QTP/UFT Within 30 Days
http://tinyurl.com/3-Tips-For-QTP-UFT

Free Webinars, Videos, and Live Trainings
http://tinyurl.com/Free-QTP-UFT-Selenium

arrName(0) = "James"
arrName(1) = "Janice"
arrName(2) = "Jane"

MsgBox LBound(arrName, 1)
'or
MsgBox LBound(arrName)

Both outputs return “0,” which is the smallest subscript.

Figure 4.5

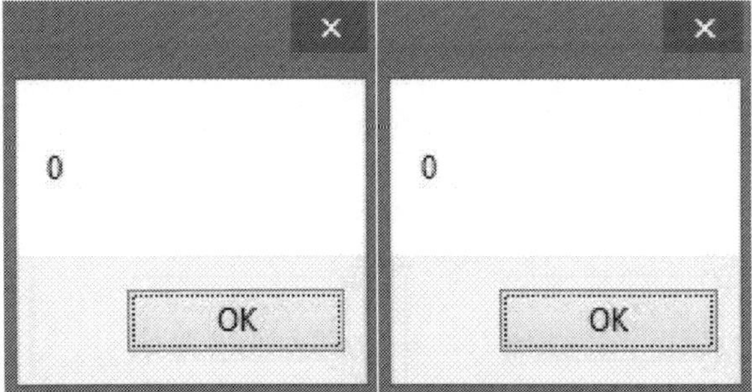

UBound

UBound is a function that returns the largest subscript for a dimension of an array. The following is an example of the UBound Function:

Syntax

UBound(NameOfArray[, Dimension])

Figure 4.6

Parameter	Description
NameOfArray	Required. An array variable name

Dimension	Optional. Basic dimensions define 1 as a column and 2 as a row. Dimensions may continue past 2. The default dimension is 1

Figure 4.7

```
Option Explicit
Dim arrName(2)

arrName(0) = "James"
arrName(1) = "Janice"
arrName(2) = "Jane"

MsgBox UBound(arrName, 1)
'or
MsgBox UBound(arrName)
```

Option Explicit
Dim arrName(2)

arrName(0) = "James"
arrName(1) = "Janice"
arrName(2) = "Jane"

MsgBox UBound(arrName, 1)
'or
MsgBox UBound(arrName)

The answer is “2,” which is the largest subscript.

Figure 4.8

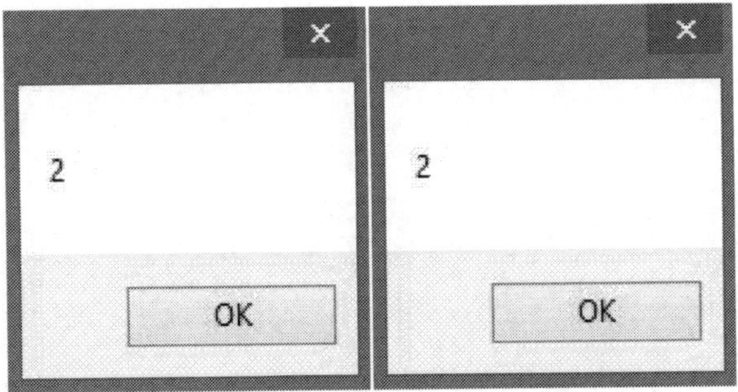

Two-Dimensional Array

Programmers must add a comma and another upper bound to declare a Two-Dimensional Array. Columns are the first dimension and rows are the second dimension. A Two-Dimensional Array displays multiple columns and multiple rows. As a result, programmers are not limited to two columns. The following is an example of a Two-Dimensional Static Array:

Dim arrName(1, 2)

Fill Two-Dimensional Array

Figure 4.9

```
'First Row
arrName(0,0) = "James"
arrName(1,0) = "Jones"

'Second Row
arrName(0,1) = "Janice"
arrName(1,1) = "Smith"

'Third Row
arrName(0,2) = "Jane"
arrName(1,2) = "Doe"
```

'First Row
arrName(0,0) = "James"
arrName(1,0) = "Jones"

'Second Row
arrName(0,1) = "Janice"
arrName(1,1) = "Smith"

'Third Row
arrName(0,2) = "Jane"
arrName(1,2) = "Doe"

Figure 4.10

	0	**1**
0	James	Jones
1	Janice	Smith
2	Jane	Doe

LBound

LBound is a function that returns the smallest subscript for a dimension of an array. The following is an example of the LBound Function using Two-Dimensional Array:

Syntax
LBound(NameOfArray[, Dimension])

Figure 4.11

Parameter	Description
NameOfArray	Required. An array variable name

Dimension	Optional. Basic dimensions define 1 as a column and 2 as a row. Dimensions may continue past 2. The default dimension is 1

Figure 4.12

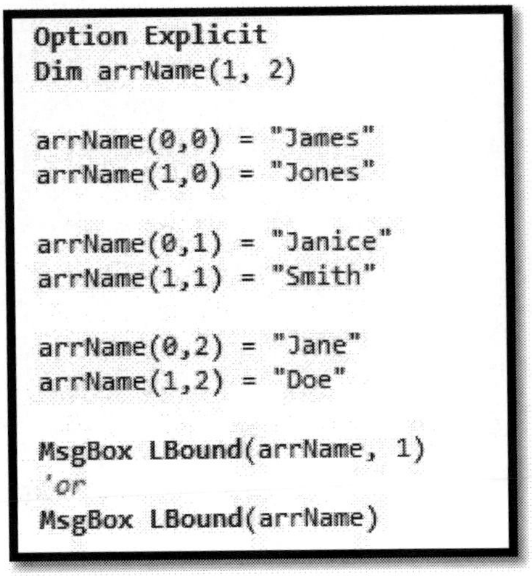

```
Option Explicit
Dim arrName(1, 2)

arrName(0,0) = "James"
arrName(1,0) = "Jones"

arrName(0,1) = "Janice"
arrName(1,1) = "Smith"

arrName(0,2) = "Jane"
arrName(1,2) = "Doe"

MsgBox LBound(arrName, 1)
'or
MsgBox LBound(arrName)
```

Option Explicit
Dim arrName(1, 2)

arrName(0,0) = "James"
arrName(1,0) = "Jones"

arrName(0,1) = "Janice"
arrName(1,1) = "Smith"

arrName(0,2) = "Jane"
arrName(1,2) = "Doe"

MsgBox LBound(arrName, 1)
'or
MsgBox LBound(arrName)

Skype: rex.jones34
Twitter: @RexJonesII
Email: Rex.Jones@Test4Success.org
LinkedIn: https://www.linkedin.com/in/rexjones34

The output returns "0," which is the smallest subscript.

Figure 4.13

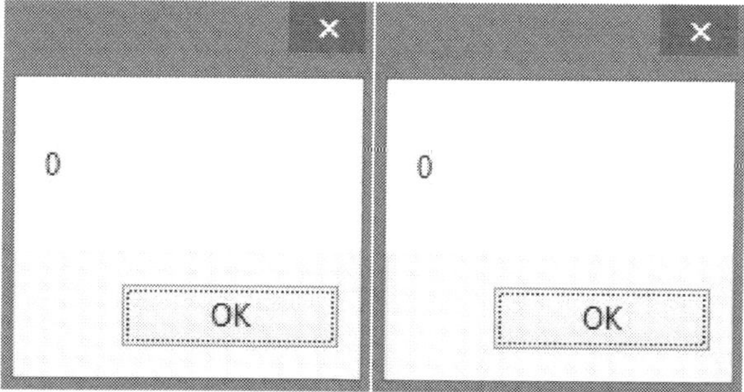

UBound

UBound is a function that returns the largest subscript for a dimension of an array. The following is an example of the UBound Function:

Syntax

UBound(NameOfArray[, Dimension])

Figure 4.14

Parameter	Description
NameOfArray	Required. An array variable name
Dimension	Optional. Basic dimensions define 1 as a column and 2 as a row. Dimensions may continue past 2. The default dimension is 1

Figure 4.15

```
Option Explicit
Dim arrName(1, 2)

arrName(0,0) = "James"
arrName(1,0) = "Jones"

arrName(0,1) = "Janice"
arrName(1,1) = "Smith"

arrName(0,2) = "Jane"
arrName(1,2) = "Doe"

MsgBox UBound(arrName, 1)
'or
MsgBox UBound(arrName)
```

Option Explicit
Dim arrName(1, 2)

arrName(0,0) = "James"
arrName(1,0) = "Jones"

arrName(0,1) = "Janice"
arrName(1,1) = "Smith"

arrName(0,2) = "Jane"
arrName(1,2) = "Doe"

MsgBox UBound(arrName, 1)
'or
MsgBox UBound(arrName)

The answer is “1,” because it is the first dimension, largest subscript.

Skype: rex.jones34
Twitter: @RexJonesII
Email: Rex.Jones@Test4Success.org
LinkedIn: https://www.linkedin.com/in/rexjones34

Figure 4.16

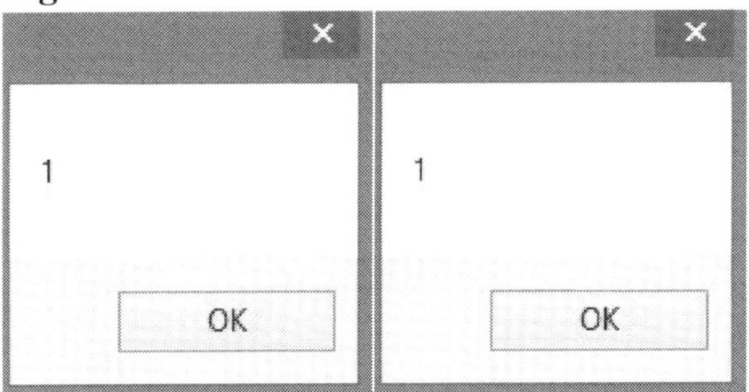

MsgBox UBound(arrName, 2)

The answer is “2” because it is the second dimension’s largest subscript.

Figure 4.17

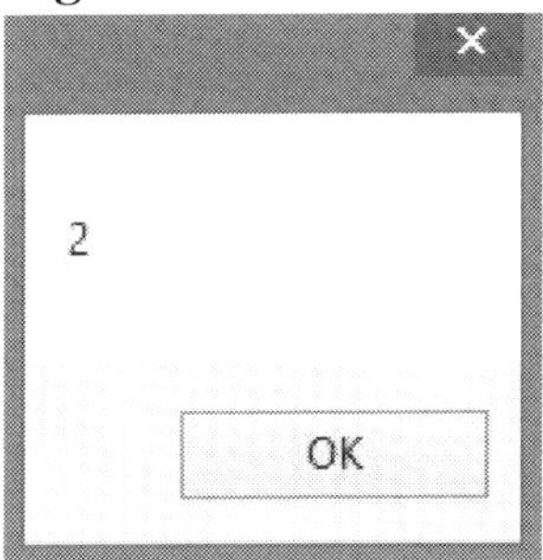

Array Function

The Array Function returns a variant containing an array. The following is an example of the Array Function:

Syntax
Array (Arglist)

Figure 4.18

3 Tips To Master QTP/UFT Within 30 Days
http://tinyurl.com/3-Tips-For-QTP-UFT

Free Webinars, Videos, and Live Trainings
http://tinyurl.com/Free-QTP-UFT-Selenium

Parameter	Description
Arglist	Required. A list (separated by commas) of values that are the element in the array

Figure 4.19

```
Option Explicit
Dim arrAge

arrAge = Array(7, 14, 21, 28, 34)
MsgBox arrAge(4)
```

Option Explicit
Dim arrAge

arrAge = **Array**(7, 14, 21, 28, 34)
MsgBox arrAge(4)

The output returns "34," because it is the fourth index.

Figure 4.20

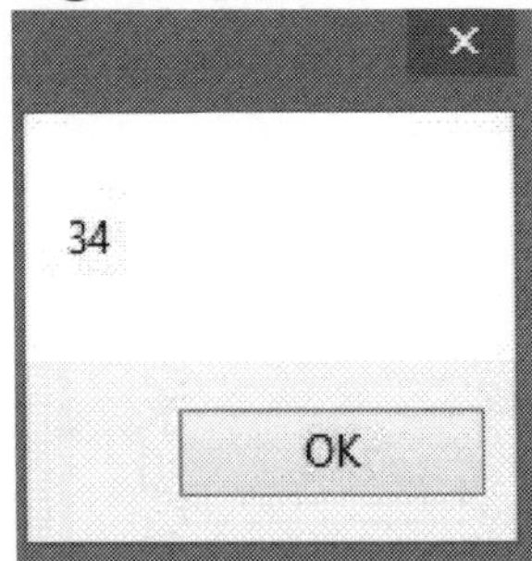

Filter Array

The Filter Function returns a zero-based array, containing a subset of a string array based on a filter criteria. The following is an example of a Filter Function:

Syntax
Filter (Inputstrings, Value[,Include, [,Compare]])

Figure 4.21

Parameter	Description
Inputstrings	Required. Search for a One-Dimensional Array of strings
Value	Optional. Search for a string
Include	Optional. A Boolean value that indicates whether to return the substrings that include or exclude the value. True returns the subset of the array that contains the value of a substring. False returns the subset of the array that does not contain the value as a substring. Default is True
Compare	Optional. Specify one of the following values to use for comparison: 0 = vbBinaryCompare: Perform a binary comparison 1 = vbTextCompare: Perform a textual comparison

Figure 4.22

```
Option Explicit
Dim arrAge, strAge
Dim i

arrAge = Array("Cat", "Dog", "Frog")
strAge = Filter(arrAge, "o")

For i = 0 To uBound(strAge)
     MsgBox strAge(i)
Next
```

Option Explicit

3 Tips To Master QTP/UFT Within 30 Days
http://tinyurl.com/3-Tips-For-QTP-UFT

Free Webinars, Videos, and Live Trainings
http://tinyurl.com/Free-QTP-UFT-Selenium

```
Dim arrAge, strAge
Dim i

arrAge = Array("Cat", "Dog", "Frog")
strAge = Filter(arrAge, "o")

For i = 0 To uBound(strAge)
   MsgBox strAge(i)
Next
```

The output returns “Dog” and “Frog,” because both have an “o.”

Figure 4.23

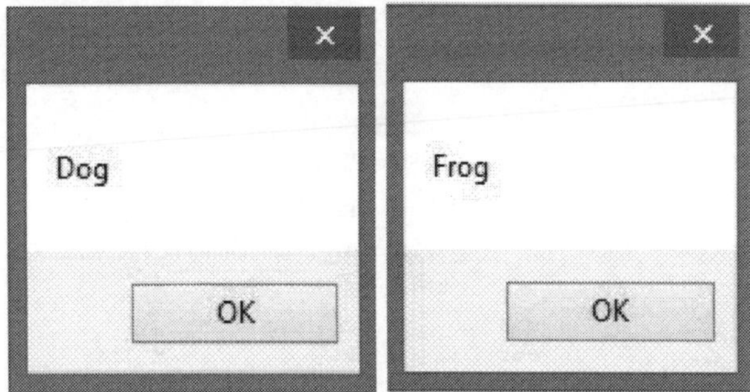

Dynamic Array Type

A Dynamic Array is available when programmers do not know the number of elements. Dynamic Arrays are not pre-constrained to upper bounds or a specific amount of dimensions. The array can be declared once, at the time it is designed, while the upper bounds and dimensions can be changed dynamically at runtime. The following is an example of a Dynamic Array:

```
Dim arrName()
```

The Dynamic Array uses a parentheses without placing upper bounds or dimensions. This informs VBScript that the programmer does not know how many elements to store in the array at design time. For example, it is not known how many rows are located in a database table. Therefore, it is not good to hardcode a specific number due to potential database changes.

Resize Arrays

Dynamic Arrays allow programmers to resize the array at runtime. The "ReDim" statement initially sets the size or changes the size of a Dynamic Array. New indexes must be filled to increase a Dynamic Array index size. In addition, the array size can be resized as many times as the programmer wants to resize the array. However, there is one caveat when using ReDim statements: All of the data previously stored in the array is lost after resizing the array. The following is an example of resizing an array:

Figure 4.24

```
Option Explicit
Dim arrAge

arrAge = Array(7, 14, 21, 28, 34)
MsgBox arrAge(4)
```

Option Explicit
Dim arrAge

arrAge = **Array**(7, 14, 21, 28, 34)
MsgBox arrAge(4)

The output returns "34."

3 Tips To Master QTP/UFT Within 30 Days
http://tinyurl.com/3-Tips-For-QTP-UFT

Free Webinars, Videos, and Live Trainings
http://tinyurl.com/Free-QTP-UFT-Selenium

Figure 4.25

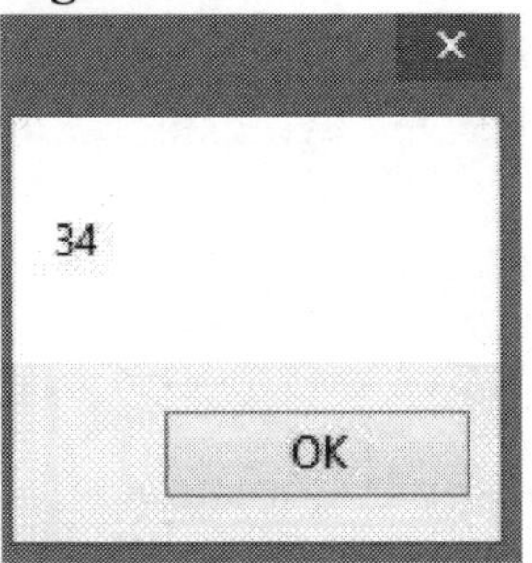

Figure 4.26

```
Option Explicit
Dim arrAge

arrAge = Array(7, 14, 21, 28, 34)
ReDim arrAge (8)
MsgBox arrAge (4)
```

Option Explicit
Dim arrAge

arrAge = **Array**(7, 14, 21, 28, 34)
ReDim arrAge (8)
MsgBox arrAge (4)

The output returns a blank value.

Skype: rex.jones34
Twitter: @RexJonesII
Email: Rex.Jones@Test4Success.org
LinkedIn: https://www.linkedin.com/in/rexjones34

Figure 4.27

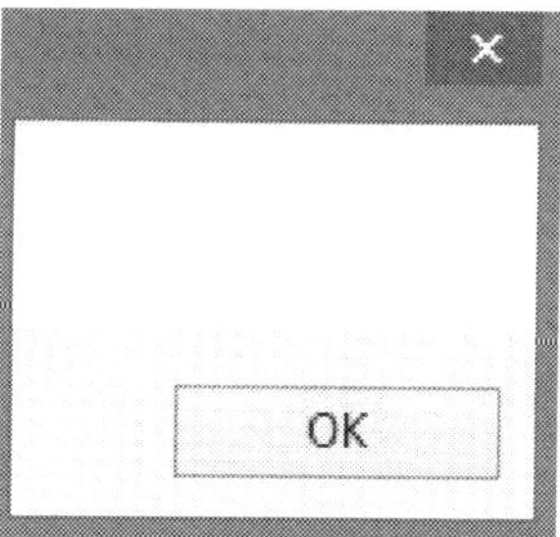

The message box will display an empty value. Sometimes it is good to lose data and other times it is not good. Use the "Preserve" keyword when it is not good to lose data. Preserve ensures the data that was previously stored in the array stays when resized. The following is an example of using the Preserve keyword:

Figure 4.28

```
Option Explicit
Dim arrAge

arrAge = Array(7, 14, 21, 28, 34)
MsgBox arrAge(4)
```

Option Explicit
Dim arrAge

arrAge = **Array**(7, 14, 21, 28, 34)
MsgBox arrAge(4)

The output returns "34."

3 Tips To Master QTP/UFT Within 30 Days
http://tinyurl.com/3-Tips-For-QTP-UFT

Free Webinars, Videos, and Live Trainings
http://tinyurl.com/Free-QTP-UFT-Selenium

Figure 4.29

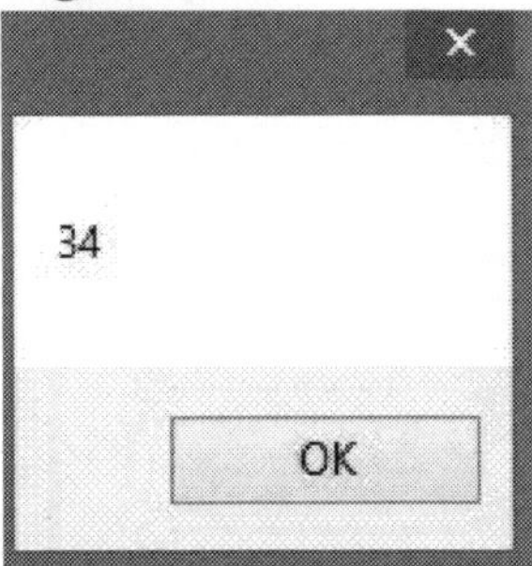

Figure 4.30

```
Option Explicit
Dim arrAge

arrAge = Array(7, 14, 21, 28, 34)
ReDim Preserve arrAge(8)
MsgBox arrAge(4)
```

Option Explicit
Dim arrAge

arrAge = **Array**(7, 14, 21, 28, 34)
ReDim Preserve arrAge(8)
MsgBox arrAge(4)

The output still returns “34.”

Skype: rex.jones34
Twitter: @RexJonesII
Email: Rex.Jones@Test4Success.org
LinkedIn: https://www.linkedin.com/in/rexjones34

Figure 4.31

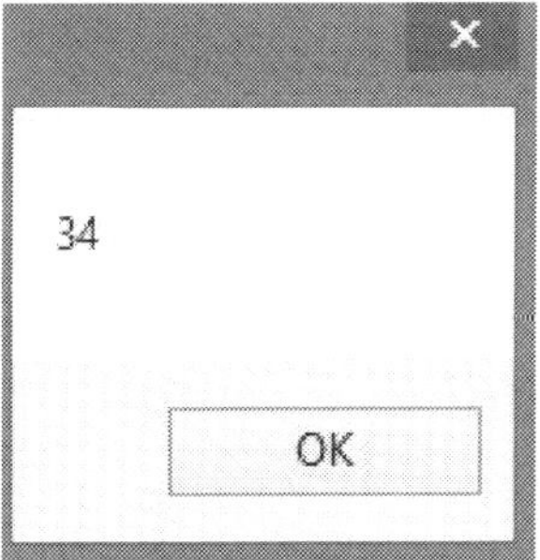

Erase Arrays

An array can be emptied by using the Erase Statement. It has different effects for Static Arrays and Dynamic Arrays. For Static Arrays, the Erase Statement erases only the item's content while the array's lower and upper bounds do not change. With a Dynamic Array, the Erase Statement completely erases an array's allocated memory. Elements are destroyed and data is deleted. The variable remains but the bounds no longer exist. Programmers must use the ReDim statement on the variable again, in order for the bounds to return. The following is an example of an Erase Statement:

Erase arrAge

Split Arrays

The Split Function allows the values of indexes in a Static or Dynamic Array to be split. It uses a delimiter to separate a string into substrings, and then assigns the substrings to an array's index. The programmer specifies the string and delimiter as an argument to the Split Function. The Split Function returns a zero-based, One-Dimensional Array that contains a specified number of substrings. The following is an example of the Split Function:

Syntax

Split (Expression[, Delimiter[, Count[, Compare]]])

---

3 Tips To Master QTP/UFT Within 30 Days
http://tinyurl.com/3-Tips-For-QTP-UFT

Free Webinars, Videos, and Live Trainings
http://tinyurl.com/Free-QTP-UFT-Selenium

Figure 4.32

Parameter	Description
Expression	An expression is a string that contains substrings and delimiters, and is required in a Split Function
Delimiter	A delimiter is a string character used to identify substring limits, and is optional in a Split Function. Space is the default
Count	The count is the number of substrings to be returned in a Split Function, and is optional. -1 indicates that all substrings are returned
Compare	Compare is optional and specifies one of the following values to use for comparison: 0 = vbBinaryCompare: Perform binary comparison 1 = vbTextCompare: Perform the textual comparison

Figure 4.33

```
Option Explicit
Dim arrColors

arrColors = Split("Black, White, Red", ",")
MsgBox arrColors(0)
```

Option Explicit
Dim arrColors

arrColors = **Split(**"Black, White, Red", ",")
MsgBox arrColors(0)

The output returns “Black,” due to index zero. Index one is “White” and index two is “Red.”

Skype: rex.jones34
Twitter: @RexJonesII
Email: Rex.Jones@Test4Success.org
LinkedIn: https://www.linkedin.com/in/rexjones34

Figure 4.34

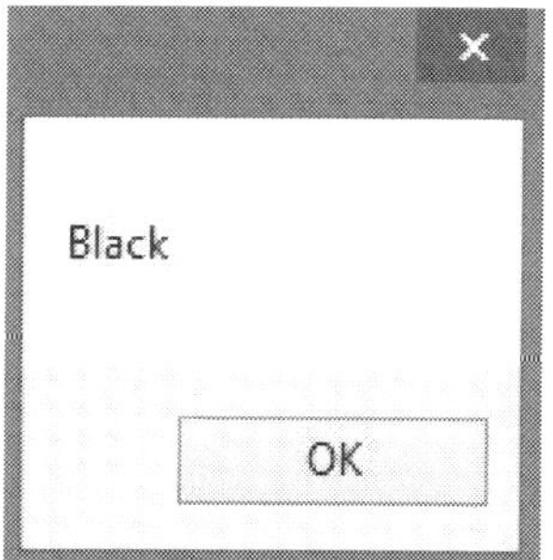

Join Arrays

The Join Function combines the substrings that each array index contains into one string and assigns that string to a variable. The variable will not be an array but a String Subtype. This function performs the reverse task of the Split Function. The following is an example of the Join Function:

Syntax
Join (List[, Delimiter])

Figure 4.35

Parameter	**Description**
List	A list is a One-Dimensional Array that contains the substrings to be joined and is required
Delimiter	A delimiter is the character(s) used to separate the substrings in the returned string in a Join Function, and is optional. Space is the default

Figure 4.36

```
Option Explicit
Dim strColors
Dim arrColors(2)

arrColors(0) = "Black"
arrColors(1) = "White"
arrColors(2) = "Red"

strColors = Join(arrColors)
MsgBox strColors
```

Option Explicit
Dim strColors
Dim arrColors(2)

arrColors(0) = "Black"
arrColors(1) = "White"
arrColors(2) = "Red"

strColors = **Join**(arrColors)
MsgBox strColors

The output returns "Black White Red" after joining the substrings in the "arrColors" indexes and assigns the result to "strColors."

Figure 4.37

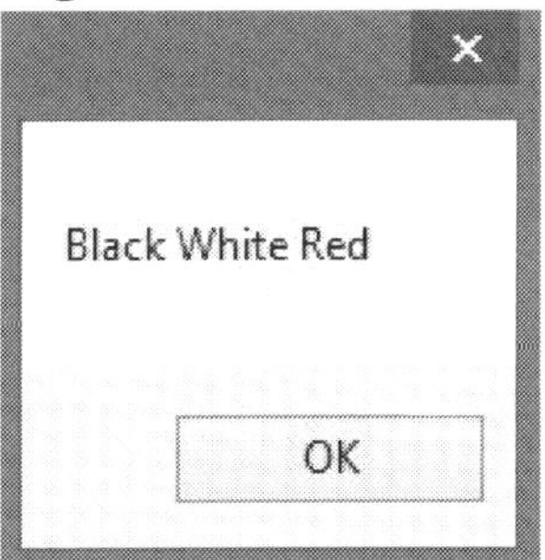

Access Arrays

Subscripts must be used to read from or write to an array element. A One-Dimensional Array is described as one element per one value. A subscript resembles the column letter and row number syntax from a spreadsheet or *x* and *y* axis. The *x* axis is a horizontal line and the *y* axis is a vertical line. Let us view examples of reading from an element and writing to an element:

Read From an Array Element

Figure 4.38

```
Option Explicit
Dim arrName(1, 2)

'First Row
arrName(0,0) = "James"
arrName(1,0) = "Jones"

'Second Row
arrName(0,1) = "Janice"
arrName(1,1) = "Smith"

'Third Row
arrName(0,2) = "Jane"
arrName(1,2) = "Doe"

MsgBox arrName(0, 0)
```

3 Tips To Master QTP/UFT Within 30 Days
http://tinyurl.com/3-Tips-For-QTP-UFT

Free Webinars, Videos, and Live Trainings
http://tinyurl.com/Free-QTP-UFT-Selenium

```
Option Explicit
Dim arrName(1, 2)

'First Row
arrName(0,0) = "James"
arrName(1,0) = "Jones"

'Second Row
arrName(0,1) = "Janice"
arrName(1,1) = "Smith"

'Third Row
arrName(0,2) = "Jane"
arrName(1,2) = "Doe"

MsgBox arrName(0, 0)
```

The output returns "James."

Figure 4.39

Write To an Array Element

Figure 4.40

```
Option Explicit
Dim arrName()

'First Row
ReDim Preserve arrName(1,0)
arrName(0,0) = "James"
arrName(1,0) = "Jones"

'Second Row
ReDim Preserve arrName(1,1)
arrName(0,1) = "Janice"
arrName(1,1) = "Smith"

'Third Row
ReDim Preserve arrName(1,2)
arrName(0,2) = "Jane"
arrName(1,2) = "Doe"

'Add 4th row
ReDim Preserve arrName(1,3)
arrName(0, 3) = "Rex"
arrName(1, 3) = "Allen"

MsgBox arrName (0,3)
```

Option Explicit
Dim arrName()

'First Row
ReDim Preserve arrName(1,0)
arrName(0,0) = "James"
arrName(1,0) = "Jones"

3 Tips To Master QTP/UFT Within 30 Days
http://tinyurl.com/3-Tips-For-QTP-UFT

Free Webinars, Videos, and Live Trainings
http://tinyurl.com/Free-QTP-UFT-Selenium

```
'Second Row
ReDim Preserve arrName(1,1)
arrName(0,1) = "Janice"
arrName(1,1) = "Smith"

'Third Row
ReDim Preserve arrName(1,2)
arrName(0,2) = "Jane"
arrName(1,2) = "Doe"

'Add 4th row
ReDim Preserve arrName(1,3)
arrName(0, 3) = "Rex"
arrName(1, 3) = "Allen"

MsgBox arrName (0,3)
```

Figure 4.41

	0	**1**
0	James	Jones
1	Janice	Doe
2	Jane	Smith
3	Rex	Allen

The output returns “Rex.” The array type changed to dynamic, while “ReDim Preserve” is added to populate the array.

Figure 4.42

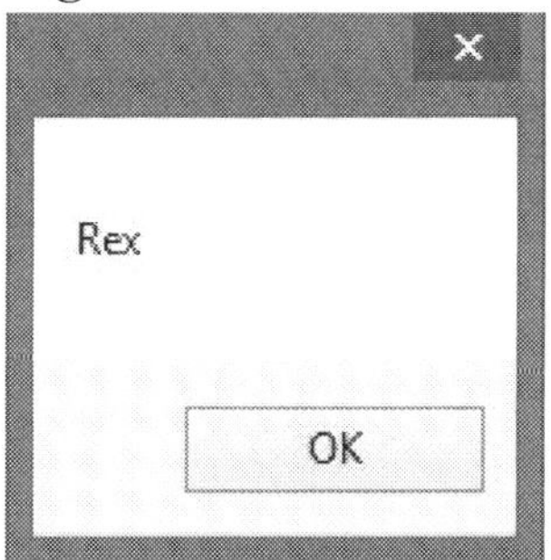

Loop-Through Arrays

The upper-bound is known when dealing with Static Arrays. It is easy to move through a Static Array because the Programmer knows how many times to iterate all of the indexes. Imagine someone wanting to view all of the items in Figure 4.43. They will not have to write the following code:

Figure 4.43

James
Janice
Jane

Figure 4.44

```
Option Explicit
Dim arrName(2)

arrName(0) = "James"
arrName(1) = "Janice"
arrName(2) = "Jane"

MsgBox arrName(0) = "James"
MsgBox arrName(1) = "Janice"
MsgBox arrName(2) = "Jane"
```

Option Explicit
Dim arrName(2)

arrName(0) = "James"
arrName(1) = "Janice"
arrName(2) = "Jane"

MsgBox arrName(0) = "James"
MsgBox arrName(1) = "Janice"
MsgBox arrName(2) = "Jane"

The first output displays “James”, second output displays “Janice”, and third output displays “Jane”

Figure 4.45

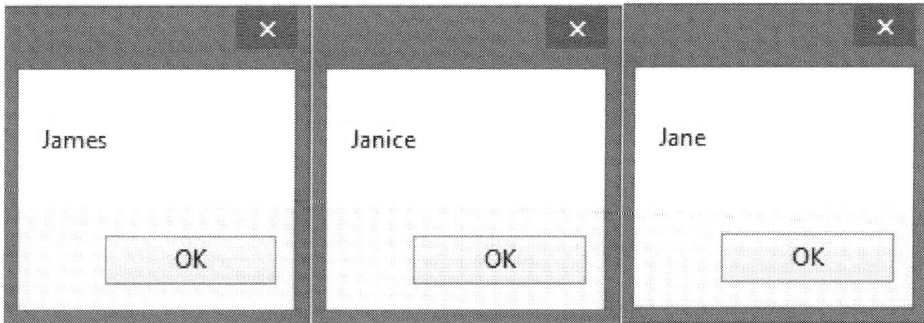

All of the items are displayed, but there is a better way to display all of the items. We can use the "For Loop," which will be explained in Chapter 5. The For Loop runs a line or group of lines of code a specific number of times. The following is an example of the For Loop to view all of the items:

Figure 4.46

```
Option Explicit
Dim i
Dim arrName(2)

arrName(0) = "James"
arrName(1) = "Janice"
arrName(2) = "Jane"

For i = 0 to 2
     MsgBox arrName(i)
Next
```

Option Explicit
Dim i
Dim arrName(2)

```
arrName(0) = "James"
arrName(1) = "Janice"
arrName(2) = "Jane"

For i = 0 to 2
   MsgBox arrName(i)
Next
```

The first output displays “James”, second output displays “Janice”, and third output displays “Jane”

Figure 4.47

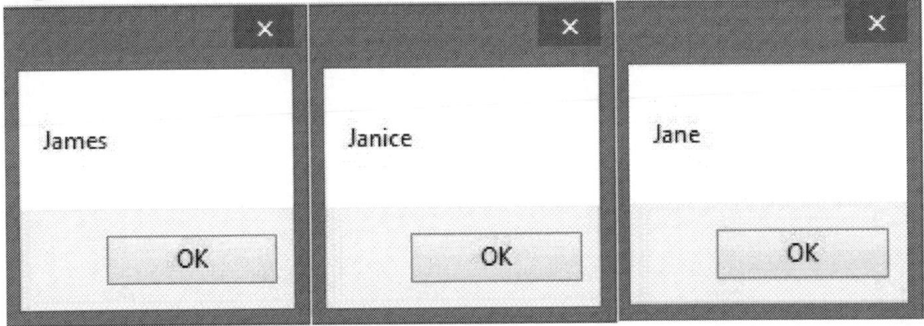

The letter “i” is a variable used to keep track of the row inside of the loop. It is represented in the “MsgBox” for each iteration. As a result, i represents the zero in the first iteration, one in the second iteration, and two in the third iteration.

In addition, LBound and UBound functions are more efficient for traversing through an array by eliminating hard-coding values. The previous example will work as follows:

Figure 4.48

```
Option Explicit
Dim i
Dim arrName(2)

arrName(0) = "James"
arrName(1) = "Janice"
arrName(2) = "Jane"

For i = LBound(arrName) to UBound(arrName)
     MsgBox arrName(i)
Next
```

Option Explicit
Dim i
Dim arrName(2)

arrName(0) = "James"
arrName(1) = "Janice"
arrName(2) = "Jane"

For i = **LBound**(arrName) **to UBound**(arrName)
  MsgBox arrName(i)
Next

The first output displays “James”, second output displays “Janice”, and third output displays “Jane”

3 Tips To Master QTP/UFT Within 30 Days
http://tinyurl.com/3-Tips-For-QTP-UFT

Free Webinars, Videos, and Live Trainings
http://tinyurl.com/Free-QTP-UFT-Selenium

Figure 4.49

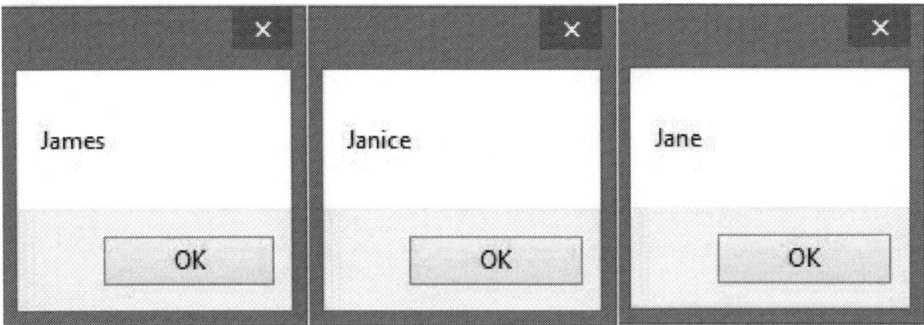

Another method for looping through arrays is the "For Each…Next Statement." The For Each…Next Statement is a loop, which repeats a group of statements for each item in an array without using LBound and UBound functions. The For Each…Next Statement will be explained in Chapter 5. The following is an example of the For Each…Next Loop:

Figure 4.50

```
Option Explicit
Dim strName
Dim arrName(2)

arrName(0) = "James"
arrName(1) = "Janice"
arrName(2) = "Jane"

For Each strName In arrName
     MsgBox strName
Next
```

Option Explicit
Dim strName
Dim arrName(2)

arrName(0) = "James"

```
arrName(1) = "Janice"
arrName(2) = "Jane"

For Each strName In arrName
    MsgBox strName
Next
```

The first output displays “James”, second output displays “Janice”, and third output displays “Jane”

Figure 4.51

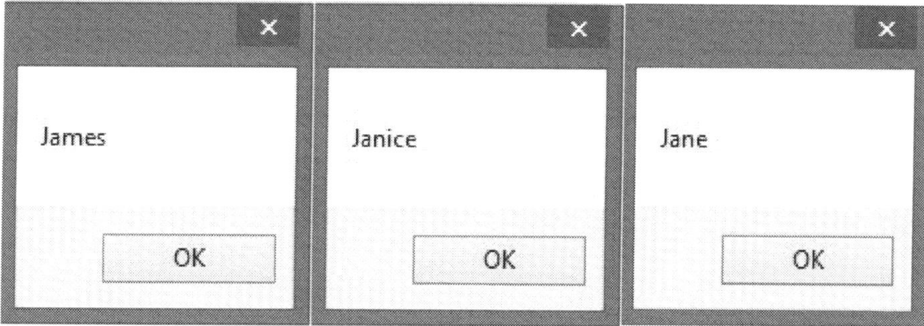

Chapter 4 went into detail regarding Arrays. Arrays can be Static or Dynamic while being read from or written to an element. Chapter 5 will explain the Flow Control’s Branching Construct and Looping Statement.

Chapter 5
Flow Control

VBScript executes from a top–down concept. It starts at the top of a script then processes one line at a time until reaching the end of the script. Logic forces some lines to be skipped due to branching, while other lines are executed more than once because of looping.

This chapter covers:

- Branching Constructs
- Looping Statements

Branching Constructs

Branching is the process of making a decision and executing one block of code based on that decision. The two constructs for branching are "If…End If" (If statement) and "Select…End Select" (Select statement). Both of the constructs are used to define a code block secured by beginning and ending statements. The If block requires a beginning statement of If and an ending statement of End If. The Select block follows a similar pattern which requires a beginning statement of Select and an ending statement of End Select. A syntax error occurs at runtime if the required statements are not entered.

"If" Block Branch

The If statement executes a set of code when a condition is True. The If statement is one of the most common structures programmers use when writing code. The following is the syntax for an If block:

Syntax
If <condition> **Then**
<statement>

End If

Anything that results in True or False can be used in place of <condition>. True or False answers are called Boolean expressions. The following is a few If construct examples:

Figure 5.1

```
Option Explicit

If 10 + 5 = 15 Then
       MsgBox "The answer is correct"
End If
```

Option Explicit

If 10 + 5 = 15 **Then**
    MsgBox "The answer is correct"
End If

The output displays "The answer is correct"

Figure 5.2

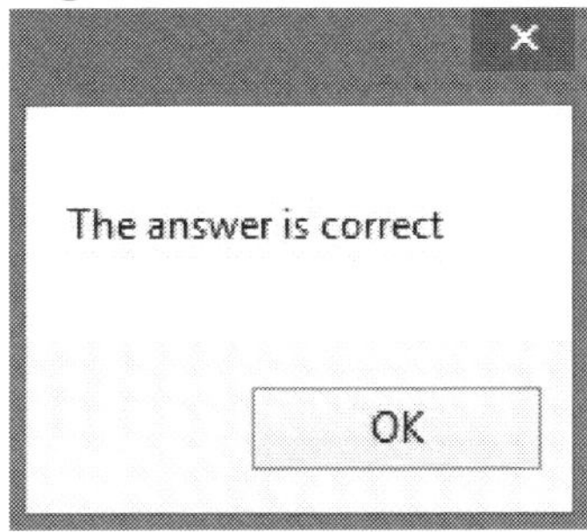

3 Tips To Master QTP/UFT Within 30 Days
http://tinyurl.com/3-Tips-For-QTP-UFT

Free Webinars, Videos, and Live Trainings
http://tinyurl.com/Free-QTP-UFT-Selenium

Figure 5.3

```
Option Explicit
Dim strFirstName

strFirstName = "Rex"

If strFirstName = "Rex"
        MsgBox "First Name " & strFirstName & " is correct"
End If
```

Option Explicit
Dim strFirstName

strFirstName = "Rex"

If strFirstName = "Rex"
    MsgBox "First Name " & strFirstName & " is correct"
End If

The output displays "First Name Rex is correct"

Figure 5.4

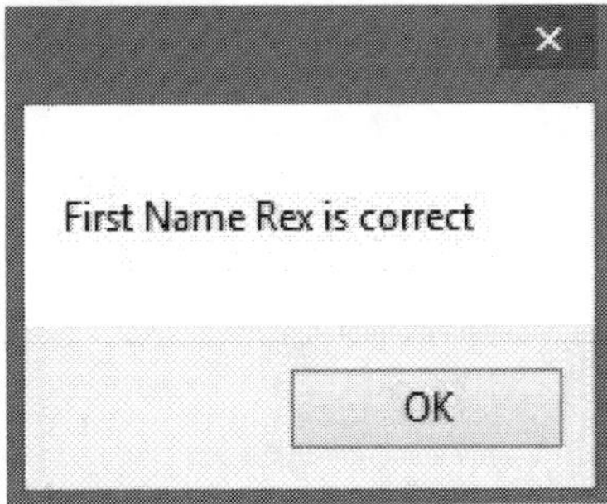

Skype: rex.jones34
Twitter: @RexJonesII
Email: Rex.Jones@Test4Success.org
LinkedIn: https://www.linkedin.com/in/rexjones34

Figure 5.5

```
Option Explicit
Dim strFirstName, strLastName

strFirstName = "Joe"
strLastName = "Doe"

If strFirstName = "Joe" and (strLastName = "Doe" or strLastName = "Blow") Then
	MsgBox "First Name is " & strFirstName & "and Last Name is " & strLastName
End If
```

```
Option Explicit
Dim strFirstName, strLastName

strFirstName = "Joe"
strLastName = "Doe"

If strFirstName = "Joe" and (strLastName = "Doe" or strLastName = "Blow") Then
    MsgBox "First Name is " & strFirstName & "and Last Name is " & strLastName
End If
```

The output displays “First Name is Joe and Last Name is Doe”

Figure 5.6

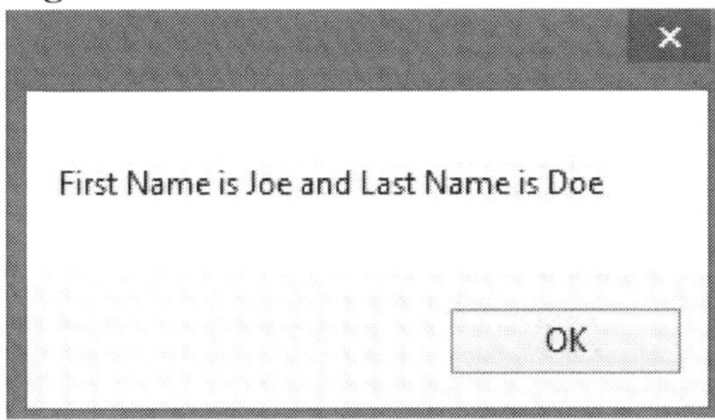

3 Tips To Master QTP/UFT Within 30 Days
http://tinyurl.com/3-Tips-For-QTP-UFT

Free Webinars, Videos, and Live Trainings
http://tinyurl.com/Free-QTP-UFT-Selenium

Else Block Branch

The “Else” block can be added as another dimension to the If construct. It will be executed if the result of the If condition is False. The following is an example of the Else block:

Syntax
If <condition> **Then**
<statement>
Else
<statement>
End If

Figure 5.7

```
Option Explicit
Dim strFirstName, strLastName

strFirstName = "James"
strLastName = "Doe"

If strFirstName = "Joe" Then
        MsgBox "First Name is " & strFirstName
Else
        MsgBox "First Name is not Joe but " & strFirstName
End If
```

```
Option Explicit
Dim strFirstName, strLastName

strFirstName = "James"
strLastName = "Doe"

If strFirstName = "Joe" Then
    MsgBox "First Name is " & strFirstName
```

Else
    MsgBox "First Name is not Joe but " & strFirstName
End If

The output displays "First Name is not Joe but James"

Figure 5.8

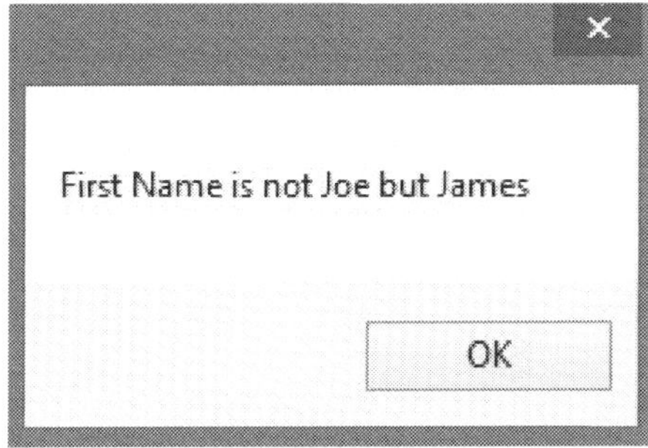

Else-If Block Branch

There are times when decisions require more than an either/or evaluation. In this case, the programmer can add several Else-If blocks. The following is an example of the Else-If block:

Syntax
If <condition> **Then**
    <statement>
ElseIf <condition> **Then**
    < statement>
ElseIf <condition> **Then**
    <statement>
Else
    <statement>
End If

---

3 Tips To Master QTP/UFT Within 30 Days
http://tinyurl.com/3-Tips-For-QTP-UFT

Free Webinars, Videos, and Live Trainings
http://tinyurl.com/Free-QTP-UFT-Selenium

Figure 5.9

```
Option Explicit
Dim strColor
strColor = "Purple"

If strColor = "Black" Then
        MsgBox "Black is a dark color"
ElseIf strColor = "Green" Then
        MsgBox "Green is a nice color"
ElseIf strColor = "Purple" Then
        MsgBox "Purple is a pretty color"
Else
        MsgBox "The color is not Black, Green, or Purple"
End If
```

Option Explicit
Dim strColor

strColor = "Purple"

If strColor = "Black" **Then**
    MsgBox "Black is a dark color"
ElseIf strColor = "Green" **Then**
    MsgBox "Green is a nice color"
ElseIf strColor = "Purple" **Then**
    MsgBox "Purple is a pretty color"
Else
    MsgBox "The color is not Black, Green, or Purple"
End If

The output displays “Purple is a pretty color”

Figure 5.10

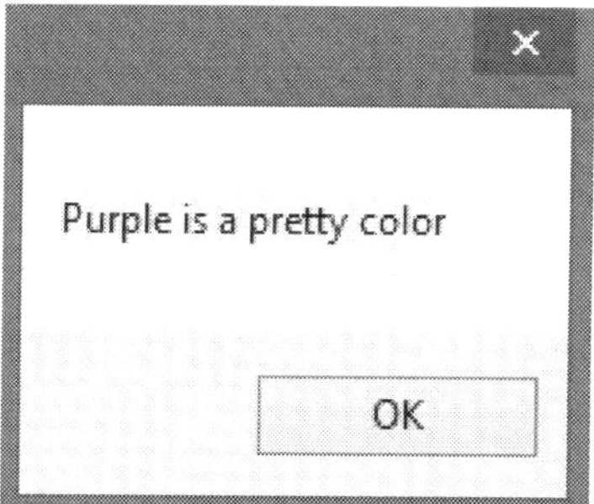

The execution moves to the first Else-If evaluation if the first condition returns False. If the first Else-If evaluation returns False, then the execution moves to the second Else-If evaluation. Finally, the execution moves to the Else block if the second Else-If evaluation returns False. Each Else-If line must end with Then, just like the If statement. The Else block is optional and always executes last. Else-If constructs are flexible because each separate Else-If line can evaluate a different expression. The following is an example of the Else-If block evaluating a unique condition without using the Else block:

Syntax

If <condition> **Then**

        <statement>

ElseIf <condition> **Then**

        <statement>

ElseIf <condition> **Then**

        <statement>

End If

---

3 Tips To Master QTP/UFT Within 30 Days
http://tinyurl.com/3-Tips-For-QTP-UFT

Free Webinars, Videos, and Live Trainings
http://tinyurl.com/Free-QTP-UFT-Selenium

Figure 5.11

```
Option Explicit
Dim intNumber

intNumber = 100

If IsNull(intNumber) Then
        MsgBox "The variable IsNull"
ElseIf IsEmpty(intNumber) Then
        MsgBox "The variable IsEmpty"
ElseIf IsNumeric(intNumber) Then
        MsgBox "The variable IsNumeric"
End If
```

Option Explicit
Dim intNumber

intNumber = 100

If IsNull(intNumber) **Then**
    MsgBox "The variable IsNull"
ElseIf IsEmpty(intNumber) **Then**
    MsgBox "The variable IsEmpty"
ElseIf IsNumeric(intNumber) **Then**
    MsgBox "The variable IsNumeric"
End If

The output displays “The variable IsNumeric”

Figure 5.12

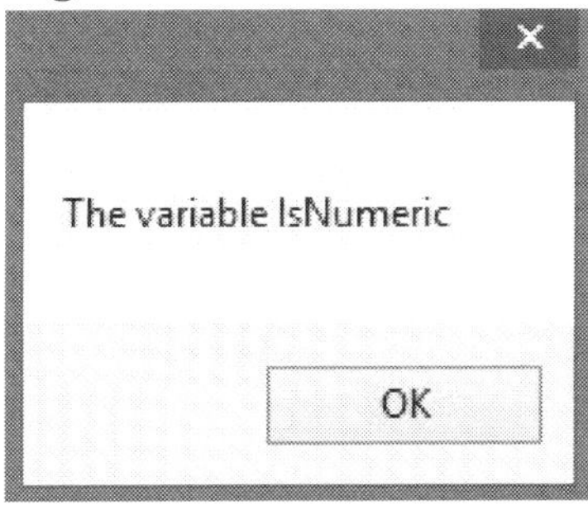

Nested If Block Branch

Programmers can add If…End If blocks within each other. The following is an example of a nested If statement:

Syntax

```
If <condition> Then
    If <condition> Then
        <statement>
    ElseIf <condition> Then
        <statement>
    ElseIf <condition> Then
        <statement>
    Else
        <statement>
    End If
Else
    <statement>
End If
```

Figure 5.13

```
Option Explicit
Dim intNumber

intNumber = 1000

If IsNumeric(intNumber) Then
        If intNumber > 0 and intNumber < 100 Then
                MsgBox "The number is greater than zero and less than 100"
        ElseIf intNumber > 100 and intNumber < 1000 Then
                MsgBox "The number is a greater than 100 and less than 1000"
        ElseIf intNumber >= 1000 Then
                MsgBox "The number is greater than or equal to 1000"
        Else
                MsgBox "The number is a negative number"
        End If
Else
        MsgBox "The variable is NOT Numeric"
End If
```

```
Option Explicit
Dim intNumber

intNumber = 1000

If IsNumeric(intNumber) Then
    If intNumber > 0 and intNumber < 100 Then
        MsgBox "The number is greater than zero and less than 100"
    ElseIf intNumber > 100 and intNumber < 1000 Then
        MsgBox "The number is a greater than 100 and less than 1000"
    ElseIf intNumber >= 1000 Then
        MsgBox "The number is greater than or equal to 1000"
    Else
        MsgBox "The number is a negative number"
    End If
```

Else
    MsgBox "The variable is NOT Numeric"
End If

The output displays "The number is greater than or equal to 1000"

Figure 5.14

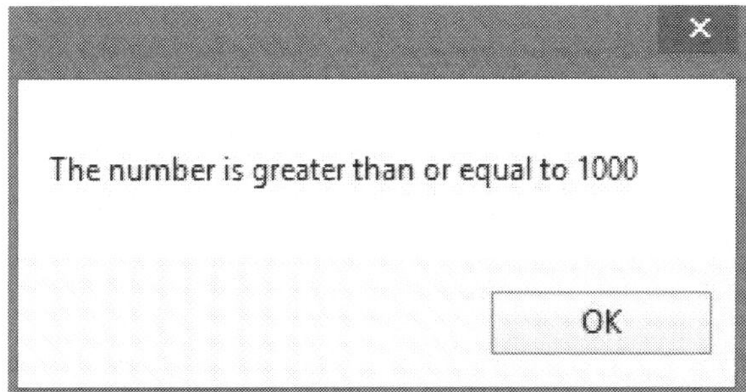

If constructs can be nested as deep as the programmer wants to nest the construct. However, the logic can become unmanageable and difficult to read if nested too deep. The concept of nesting to deep is subjective and based upon what the individual programmer or programming team deems as too deep for their specific project.

Select Case Block Branch

The Select…End Select construct is helpful when evaluating different possible outcomes for the same condition. As a result, the Select statement is an alternative to the If…End If block with several Else-If evaluations. Implementing the Select statement is more efficient than the Else-If statement in certain cases because every expression for Else-If is evaluated, whereas the Select …End Select is evaluated only one time. Select blocks can only be used when evaluating different variations of the same expressions. The following is the syntax for a Select Case statement:

Syntax
Select Case <condition>

Case <1st possibility>
<statement>
Case <2nd possibility>
<statement>
Case <3rd possibility>
<statement>
Case <n possibility>
<statement>
Case Else
<statement>
End Select

Figure 5.15

```
Option Explicit
Dim strColor

strColor = "Purple"

Select Case strColor
        Case "Black"
                MsgBox "Black is a dark color"
        Case "Green"
                MsgBox "Green is a nice color"
        Case "Purple"
                MsgBox "Purple is a pretty color"
        Case Else
                MsgBox "The color is not Black, Green, or Purple"
End Select
```

Option Explicit
Dim strColor

Skype: rex.jones34
Twitter: @RexJonesII
Email: Rex.Jones@Test4Success.org
LinkedIn: https://www.linkedin.com/in/rexjones34

```
strColor = "Purple"

Select Case strColor
    Case "Black"
        MsgBox "Black is a dark color"
    Case "Green"
        MsgBox "Green is a nice color"
    Case "Purple"
        MsgBox "Purple is a pretty color"
    Case Else
        MsgBox "The color is not Black, Green, or Purple"
End Select
```

The output displays "Purple is a pretty color"

Figure 5.16

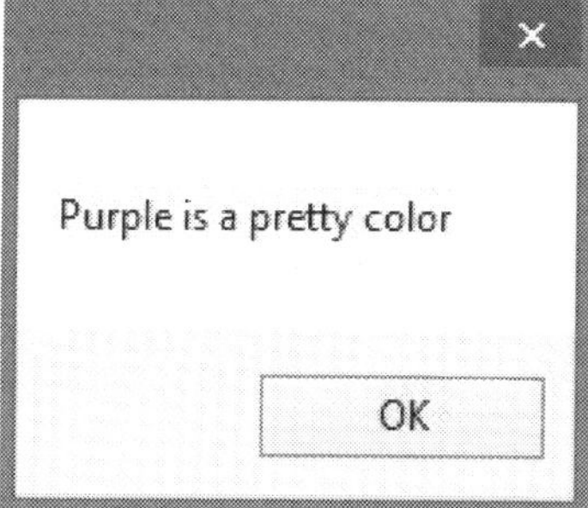

The first line evaluates the condition "strColor." Then the Case statements check for possibilities. Finally, always consider the "Case Else" block, even though it is optional. It will be executed if none of the possibilities return True. There are two reasons for adding the optional Case Else block:

1. To add documentation to the code explaining why it should not be executed, or
2. To catch unexpected changes to the programmer's code or input data

"Nested Select Case" Block Branch

The Select…End Select blocks can be nested within one another. In addition, programmers can nest If…End If blocks inside the Select …End Select block. The following is a nested Select Case block:

Syntax

```
Select Case <condition>
    Case <1st possibility>
        Select Case <condition>
            Case <1st possibility>
                If <condition> Then
                    <statement>
                Else
                    <statement>
                End If
            Case <2nd possibility>
                <statement>
            Case <3rd possibility>
                <statement>
            Case Else
                <statement>
        End Select
    Case <2nd possibility>
        <statement>
    Case <3rd possibility>
        <statement>
    Case Else
        <statement>
End Select
```

Skype: rex.jones34
Twitter: @RexJonesII
Email: Rex.Jones@Test4Success.org
LinkedIn: https://www.linkedin.com/in/rexjones34

Figure 5.17

```
Option Explicit
Dim strColor, strBlack

strColor = "Black"
strBlack = "Light Black"

Select Case strColor
	Case "Black"
		Select Case strBlack
			Case "Light Black"
				If strBlack = "Light Black" Then
					MsgBox "The color is Light Black and looks gray / grey"
				Else
					MsgBox "The color is not Light Black"
				End If
			Case "Medium Black"
				MsgBox "The color is in between Light and Dark Black"
			Case "Dark Black"
				MsgBox "The color is Dark Black"
			Case Else
				MsgBox "The color is not Black"
		End Select
	Case "Green"
		MsgBox "Green is a nice color"
	Case "Purple"
		MsgBox "Purple is a pretty color"
	Case Else
		MsgBox "The color is not Black, Green, or Purple"
End Select
```

Option Explicit
Dim strColor, strBlack

strColor = "Black"
strBlack = "Light Black"

Select Case strColor
    Case "Black"
        Select Case strBlack
            Case "Light Black"

```
                If strBlack = "Light Black" Then
                    MsgBox "The color is Light Black and looks gray / grey"
                Else
                    MsgBox "The color is not Light Black"
                End If
            Case "Medium Black"
                MsgBox "The color is in between Light and Dark Black"
            Case "Dark Black"
                MsgBox "The color is Dark Black"
            Case Else
                MsgBox "The color is not Black"
        End Select
    Case "Green"
        MsgBox "Green is a nice color"
    Case "Purple"
        MsgBox "Purple is a pretty color"
    Case Else
        MsgBox "The color is not Black, Green, or Purple"
End Select
```

The output displays “The color is Light Black and looks gray / grey”

Figure 5.18

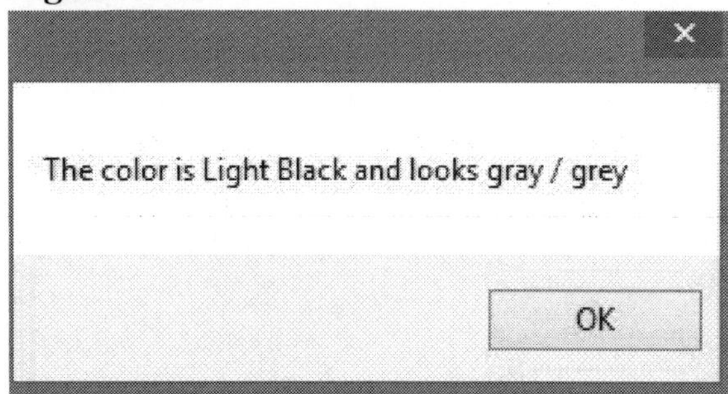

Looping Statements

Looping is the process of repeating the same block of code. VBScript has four looping statements that are used in different circumstances. The four looping statements are:

1. For…Next Statement
2. For Each…Next Statement
3. Do…Loop Statement
4. While…Wend Statement

Although there are four looping statements, the While…Wend Statement has descended from popularity. The While…Wend Statement works without a problem, but has been replaced by the Do…Loop Statement. Do…Loop Statements perform the same function as the While…Wend Statement. However, the Do…Loop Statement is more versatile because it has keywords (While and Until) and can break out of the loop by using an "Exit Do" statement. This section will focus on three of the four looping statements.

For…Next Statement

The For…Next loop repeats a group of statements a finite number of times. The following is an example of the For…Next syntax:

Syntax
For Iterator = StartValue **To** EndValue (**Step** StepExpression)
    <statement>
    (Exit For)
Next

Figure 5.19

Arguments	Description

Iterator	A variable that is used as a loop iterator
StartValue	The starting value of the iterator
EndValue	The ending value of the iterator
StepExpression	The iterator changes after every loop according to the step expression value. Default value is one.
Statement	A statement or statements that are executed
Exit For	Forces a break out of the loop

Figure 5.20

```
Option Explicit
Dim intNumber

For intNumber = 1 To 6 Step 2
        MsgBox "Iterator Value: " & intNumber
Next
```

Option Explicit
Dim intNumber

For intNumber = 1 **To** 6 **Step** 2
    MsgBox "Iterator Value: " & intNumber
Next

The first output displays “Iterator Value: 1,” the second output displays “Iterator Value: 3,” and the third output displays “Iterator Value: 5.”

Figure 5.21

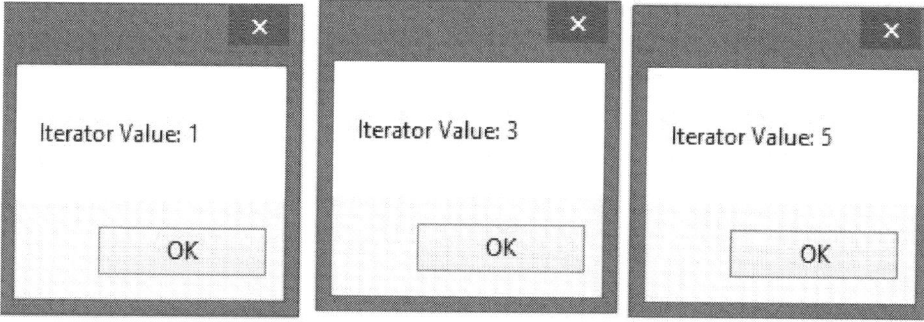

The For block specifies the iterator loop variable "intNumber," a start value of one, an end value of six, and a numeric step expression. ". Consequently, the Next block is increased by the step expression, which is "2" in the example. The step expression allows VBScript to skip numbers two, four, and six while selecting one, three, and five. The step expression also allows VBScript to decrease the iterator value by using a negative number, causing the loop to go backwards. It is important to make the end value less than the start value when using a negative number. The following is an example of a negative step expression:

Figure 5.22

```
Option Explicit
Dim intNumber

For intNumber = 6 To 1 Step -2
      MsgBox "Iterator Value: " & intNumber
Next
```

Option Explicit
Dim intNumber

For intNumber = 6 **To** 1 **Step** -2

3 Tips To Master QTP/UFT Within 30 Days
http://tinyurl.com/3-Tips-For-QTP-UFT

Free Webinars, Videos, and Live Trainings
http://tinyurl.com/Free-QTP-UFT-Selenium

MsgBox "Iterator Value: " & intNumber
Next

The first output displays “Iterator Value: 6,” the second output displays “Iterator Value: 4,” and the third output displays “Iterator Value: 2.”

Figure 5.23

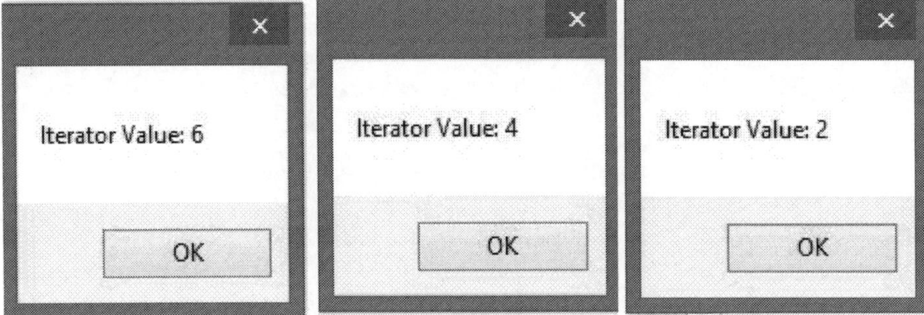

The step expression is optional, but defaults to one if it is omitted. The following is an example of the For Loop without the step expression:

Figure 5.24

```
Option Explicit
Dim intNumber

For intNumber = 0 To 2
        MsgBox "Iterator Value: " & intNumber
Next
```

Option Explicit
Dim intNumber

For intNumber = 0 **To** 2

Skype: rex.jones34
Twitter: @RexJonesII
Email: Rex.Jones@Test4Success.org
LinkedIn: https://www.linkedin.com/in/rexjones34

```
    MsgBox "Iterator Value: " & intNumber
Next
```

The first output displays “Iterator Value: 0,” the second output displays “Iterator Value: 1,” and the third output displays “Iterator Value: 2.”

Figure 5.25

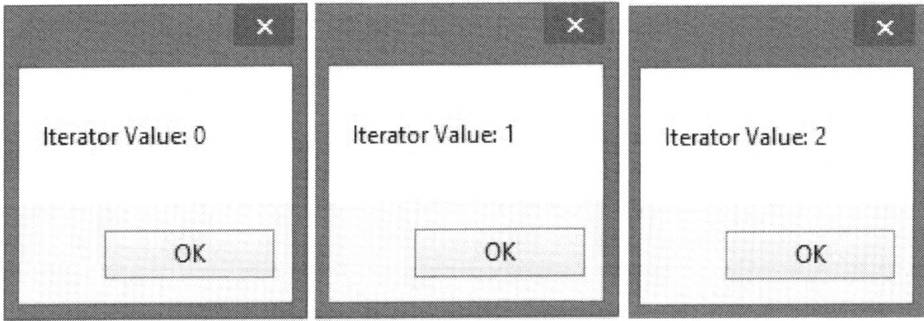

The loop condition “intNumber = 0 **To** 2” means that the loop will execute three times starting from zero, moving to one, and finally ending with two. The loop will stop after looping the third time. Note from the previous examples that the loop variable can start at any number (0, 1, and 6). The loop can also include a negative value. The following is an example of a loop variable starting with a negative number:

Figure 5.26

```
Option Explicit
Dim intNumber

For intNumber = -34 To -100 Step -25
        MsgBox "Iterator Value: " & intNumber
Next
```

Option Explicit
Dim intNumber

For intNumber = -34 **To** -100 **Step** -25
    MsgBox "Iterator Value: " & intNumber
Next

The output displays "Iterator Value: -34, Iterator Value: -59, and Iterator Value: -84."

Figure 5.27

Exit For Statement transfers control out of the For Loop and jumps to the next line after the Next Statement. The following is an example of the Exit For Statement:

Figure 5.28

```
Option Explicit
Dim intNumber

For intNumber = -34 To -100 Step -25
        MsgBox "Iterator Value: " & intNumber
        Exit For
Next

MsgBox "The Exit For statement jumped out of the For Loop and did not display -59 and -84."
```

```
Option Explicit
Dim intNumber

For intNumber = -34 To -100 Step -25
    MsgBox "Iterator Value: " & intNumber
    Exit For
Next
MsgBox "The Exit For statement jumped out of the For Loop and did not display -59 and -84."
```

The first output displays “Iterator Value: -34” and the second output displays “The Exit For statement jumped out of the For Loop and did not display -59 and -84.”

Figure 5.29

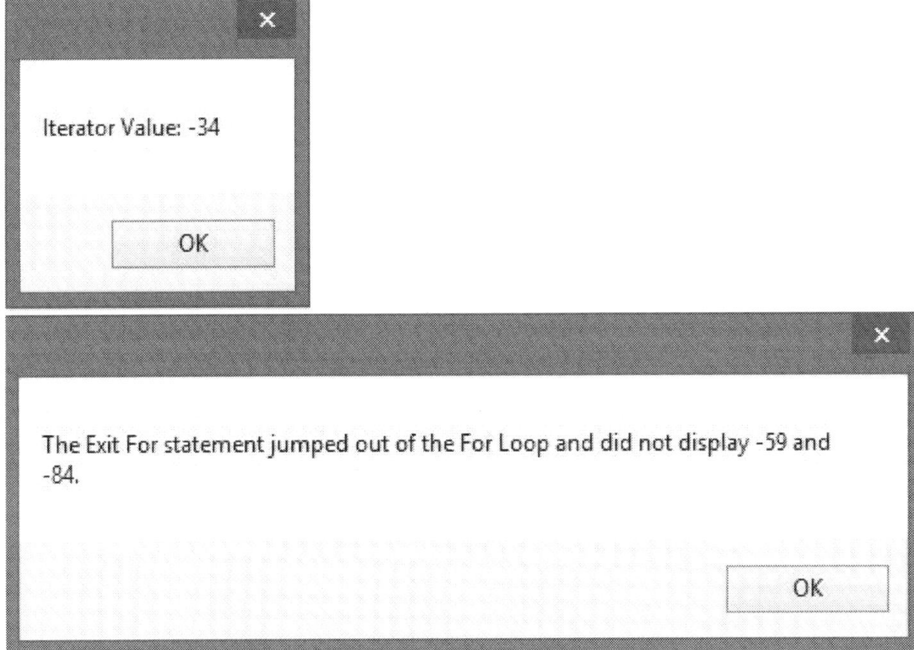

3 Tips To Master QTP/UFT Within 30 Days
http://tinyurl.com/3-Tips-For-QTP-UFT

Free Webinars, Videos, and Live Trainings
http://tinyurl.com/Free-QTP-UFT-Selenium

For Each…Next Statement

The For Each…Next Statement is a special loop that is used for traversing collections. A collection is an accumulation of data. Collections can be any kind of data but normally they consist of objects of the same type. The loop executes each element in the group. An iterator is not used in the For Each…Next Statement. Hence, programmers cannot control how many times the loop will run. Looping depends upon the number of objects in the collection. The For Each…Next Statement is mainly used with arrays or FileSystemObject (FSO).

Arrays were covered in Chapter 4 *(see FSO in Chapter 3 "Part 2 - You Must Learn VBScript for QTP – UFT".)* The following is the For Each…Next" Statement syntax:

Syntax
For Each object **In** Group
<statement>
(Exit For)
<statement>
Next

Figure 5.30

Arguments	**Description**
Object	A variable that iterates through all of the objects in a collection or array.
Group	The name of a collection or array
Statement	A statement or statements that executes every object in a specified group
Exit For	Forces a break out of the loop

Skype: rex.jones34
Twitter: @RexJonesII
Email: Rex.Jones@Test4Success.org
LinkedIn: https://www.linkedin.com/in/rexjones34

Figure 5.31

```
Option Explicit
Dim arrNames, strName

arrNames = Array("James", "John", "Joe")

For Each strName In arrNames
       MsgBox "Name is " & strName
Next
```

Option Explicit
Dim arrNames, strName

arrNames = **Array**("James", "John", "Joe")

For Each strName **In** arrNames
    MsgBox "Name is " & strName
Next

The first output displays "Name is James," the second output displays "Name is John," and the third output displays "Name is Joe."

Figure 5.32

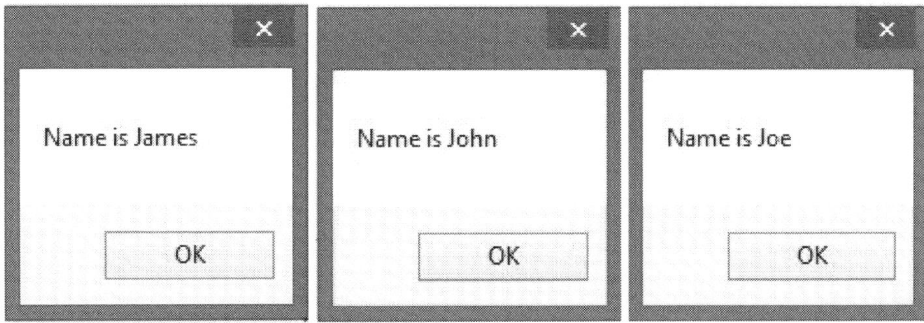

The arrNames group is a collection of strName objects. Therefore, the code is stating view each strName object in the arrNames group. The variable strName holds a reference to each name in the arrNames group. If the arrNames group is empty, then the loop will not execute. Exit For is optional, but can be useful for terminating the looping process. The following is an example of the For Each…Next statement using the Exit For part:

Figure 5.33

```
Option Explicit
Dim arrNames, strName

arrNames = Array("James", "John", "Joe")

For Each strName In arrNames
        MsgBox "Name is " & strName

        If strName = "John" Then
                MsgBox "Loop exits when Name equals " & strName
                Exit For
        End If
Next
MsgBox "Found the name we were looking for"
```

Option Explicit
Dim arrNames, strName

arrNames = **Array**("James", "John", "Joe")

For Each strName **In** arrNames
    MsgBox "Name is " & strName

    If strName = "John" **Then**
        MsgBox "Loop exits when Name equals " & strName
        Exit For

```
    End If
Next
MsgBox "Found the name we were looking for"
```

The first output displays "Name is James," the second output displays "Name is John," the third output displays "Loop exits when Name equals John," and the fourth output displays "Found the name we were looking for." The Exit For Statement terminates the For Loop and jumps to the line after the Next Statement when locating a specific name "John." The name "Joe" is not displayed like the previous example when Exit For was not used.

Figure 5.34

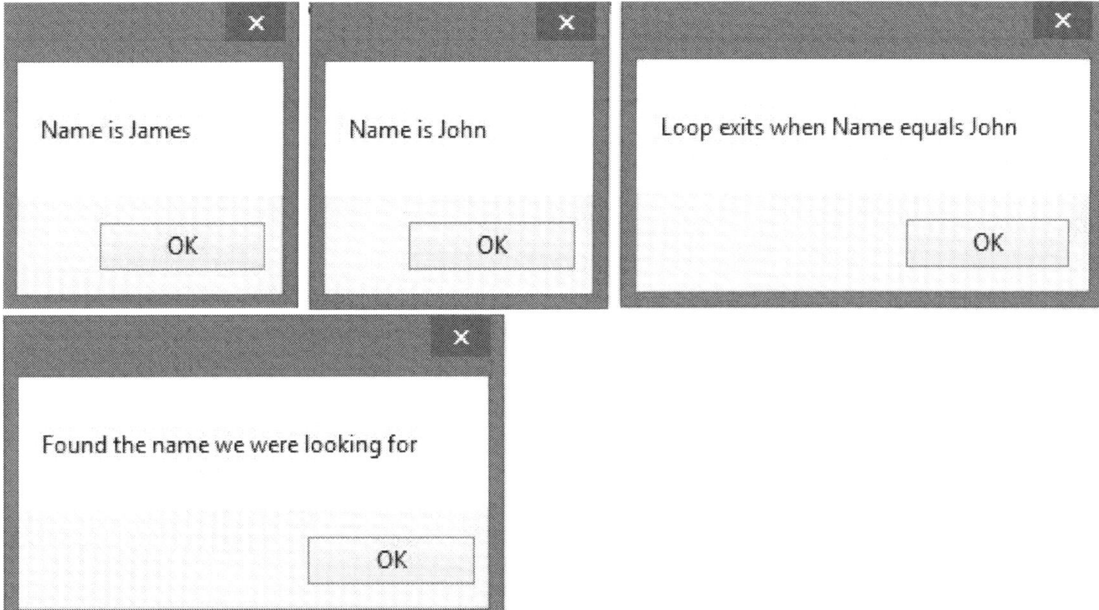

Do…Loop Statement

The Do…Loop Statement is capable of many uses due to its keywords "While" or "Until." The Do…Loop executes based on any criteria using keywords While or Until. The block of statements are repeated while a condition is True or until a condition becomes True. The keywords can be used at the beginning or end of the loop to control the number of loops executed.

There is a Do Statement that sets the beginning of a block and a Loop Statement that specifies the end of a block. Placing a condition on the Do statement with a keyword allows the script to decide whether or not to execute a statement. However, placing a condition on the Loop Statement guarantees the statement will be executed at least one time.

The Do Loop has an optional "Exit Do" Statement. Like the Exit For Statement, the Exit Do Statement transfers control out of a loop. The code breaks out of the loop to the line after the Do Loop block.

Do While

The While keyword repeats a block of statements while a condition is True. The following is the syntax for the Do While…Loop and Do… Loop While:

Syntax
Do While condition
<statement>
(Exit Do)
<statement>
Loop

Figure 5.35

Arguments	Description
Do	A required argument that starts the Do Loop
While	A required argument that indicates the loop continues while the condition is True
Condition	An expression that is True or False. Null conditions are treated as False

Statement	A statement is repeated while a condition is True
Exit Do	Forces a break out of the loop
Loop	A required argument that ends the Do Loop definition

Figure 5.36

```
Option Explicit
Dim i

i = 3

Do While i < 3
        MsgBox "Iterator = " & i
        i = i + 1
Loop

MsgBox "Iterator is 3 or more"
```

```
Option Explicit
Dim i

i = 3

Do While i < 3
    MsgBox "Iterator = " & i
    i = i + 1
Loop

MsgBox "Iterator is 3 or more"
```

The output displays “Iterator is 3 or more”

3 Tips To Master QTP/UFT Within 30 Days
http://tinyurl.com/3-Tips-For-QTP-UFT

Free Webinars, Videos, and Live Trainings
http://tinyurl.com/Free-QTP-UFT-Selenium

Figure 5.37

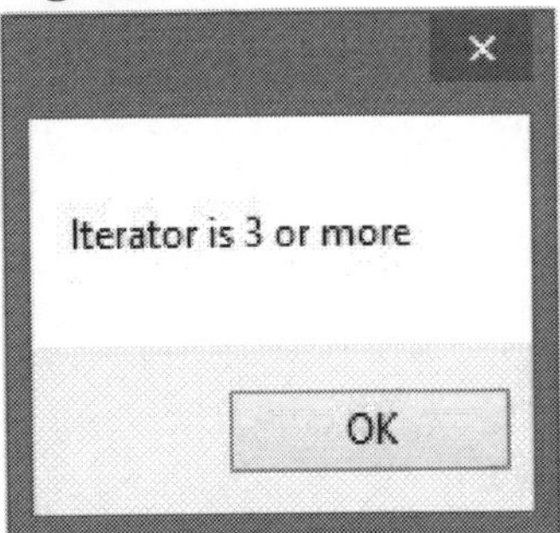

The loop has a condition with the Do Statement. For this reason, the statement is executed if the decision returns True. In this case, it returns False after setting i to three with the statement "i = 3." The condition "**Do While** i < 3" will not execute because i which equals three, is not less than three. The following is an example of the Do While…Loop flowchart:

Figure 5.38

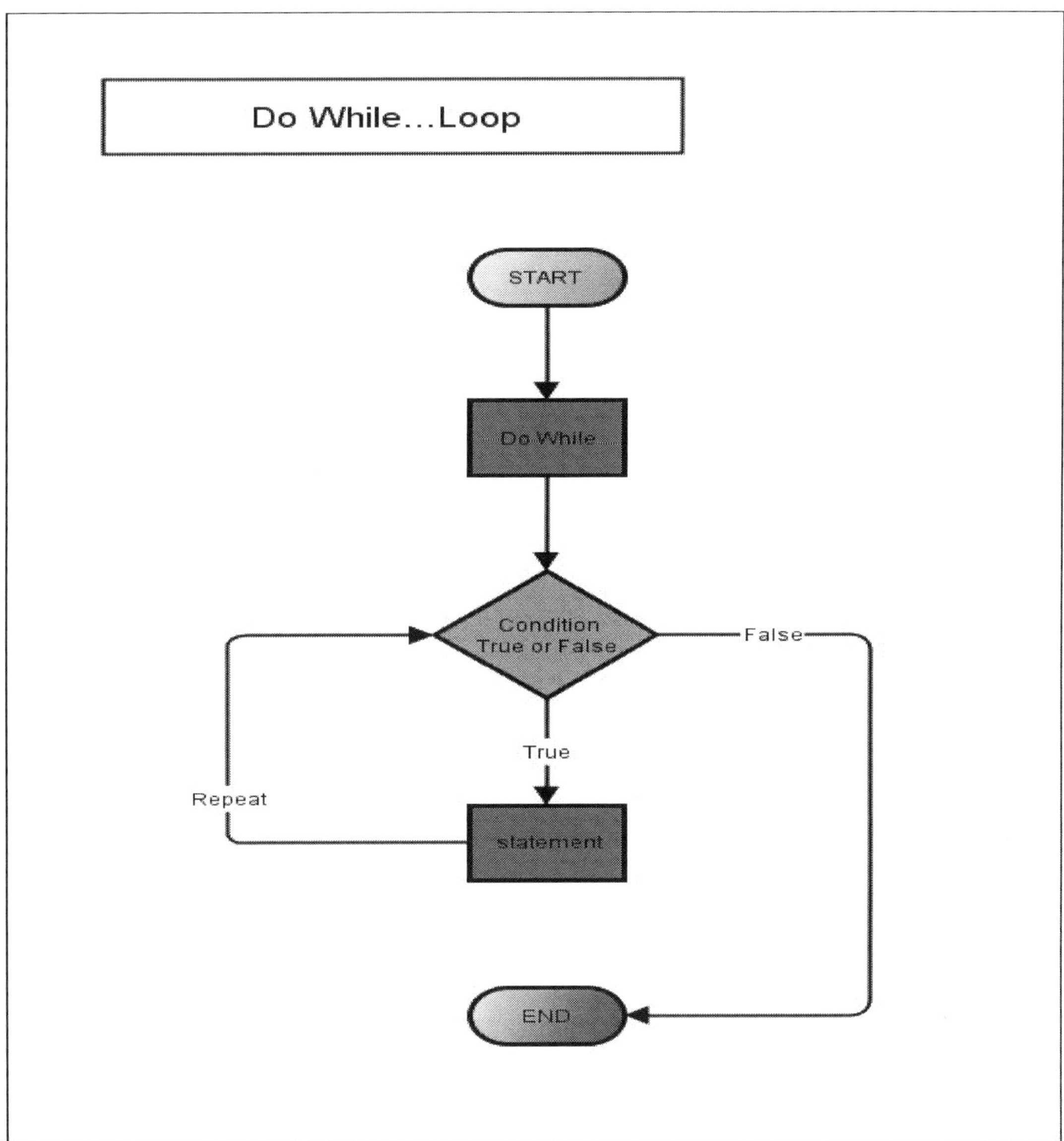
Do While...Loop
START
Do While
Condition
True or False
False
True
Repeat
statement
END

Syntax

Do

<statement>

(Exit Do)

<statement>

Loop While condition

Figure 5.39

```
Option Explicit
Dim i

i = 3

Do
        MsgBox "Iterator = " & i
        i = i + 1
Loop While i < 3

MsgBox "Iterator is 3 or more"
```

Option Explicit
Dim i

i = 3

Do
MsgBox "Iterator = " & i
i = i + 1
Loop While i < 3

Skype: rex.jones34
Twitter: @RexJonesII
Email: Rex.Jones@Test4Success.org
LinkedIn: https://www.linkedin.com/in/rexjones34

MsgBox "Iterator is 3 or more"

The output displays “Iterator = 3” and “Iterator is 3 or more”

Figure 5.40

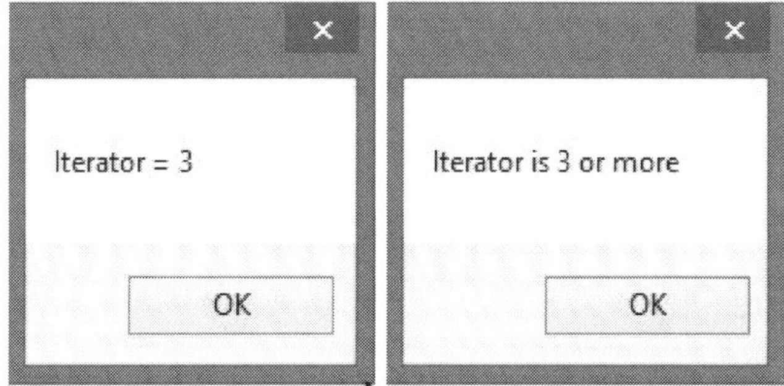

The statement is executed automatically at least one time because there is a condition on the Loop Statement. The iterator equals three by setting i to 3 (i = 3) that produces the first output (Iterator = 3) by way of statement (**MsgBox** "Iterator = " & i). The iterator increases to four with statement “i = i + 1.” Condition “**Loop While** i < 3” causes the loop to stop because four is not less than three, which displays the second output: “Iterator is 3 or more.” The following is an example of the Do…Loop While flowchart:

Figure 5.41

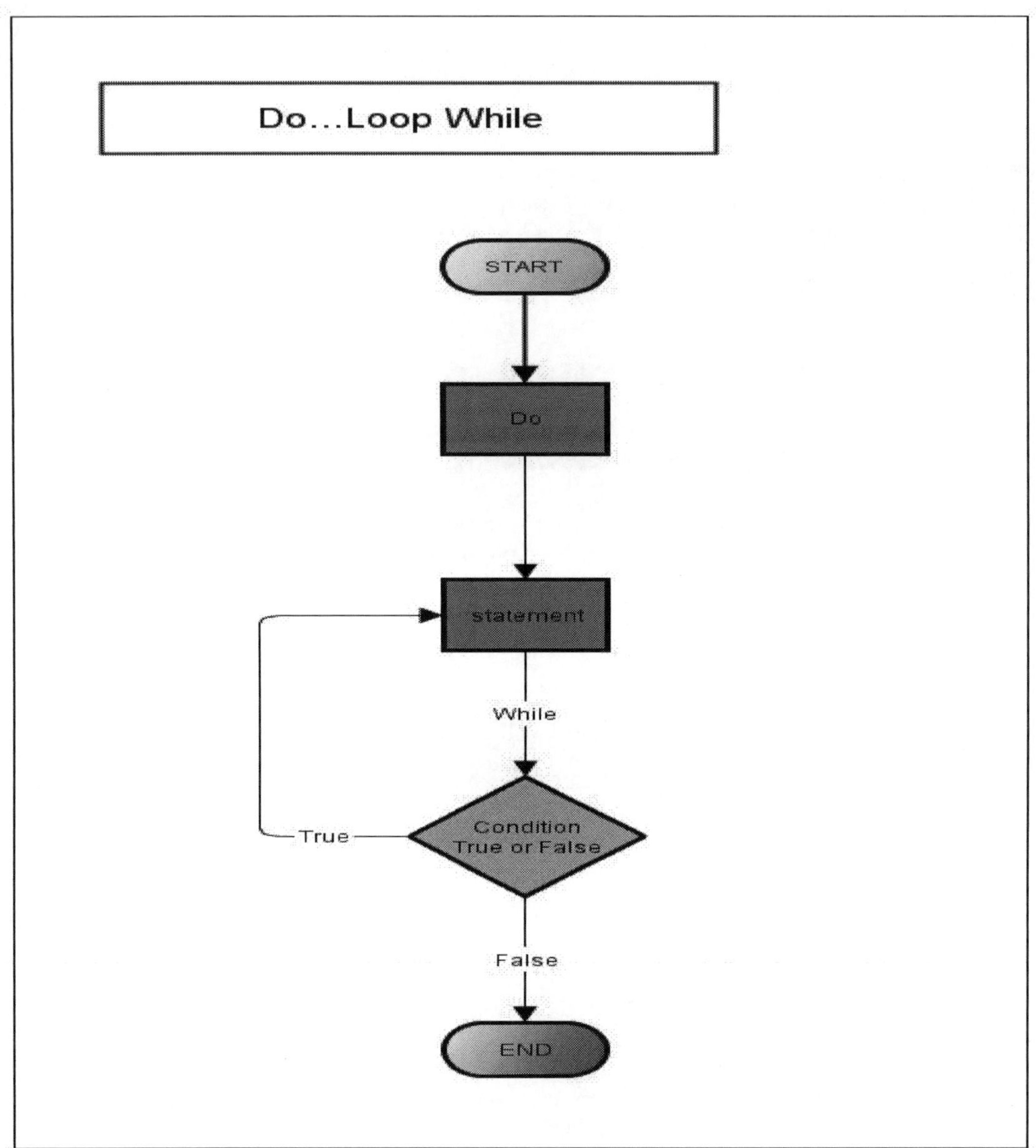

Skype: rex.jones34
Twitter: @RexJonesII
Email: Rex.Jones@Test4Success.org
LinkedIn: https://www.linkedin.com/in/rexjones34

Do Until

The Until keyword repeats a block of statements as long as the condition is False. In other words, the statements are repeated until a condition becomes True. The following is the syntax for the Do Until…Loop and Do…Loop Until:

Syntax
Do Until condition
<statement>
(Exit Do)
<statement>
Loop

Figure 5.42

Arguments	Description
Do	A required argument that starts the Do Loop
Until	A required argument that indicates the loop continues until the condition becomes True
Condition	An expression that is True or False. Null conditions are treated as False
Statement	A statement is repeated until a condition becomes True
Exit Do	Forces a break out of the loop
Loop	A required argument that ends the Do Loop definition

Figure 5.43

```
Option Explicit
Dim i

i = 1

Do Until i < 3
        MsgBox "Iterator = " & i
        i = i + 1
Loop

MsgBox "Iterator is less than 3"
```

Option Explicit
Dim i

i = 1

Do Until i < 3
    MsgBox "Iterator = " & i
    i = i + 1
Loop

MsgBox "Iterator is less than 3"

The output displays "Iterator is less than 3"

Figure 5.44

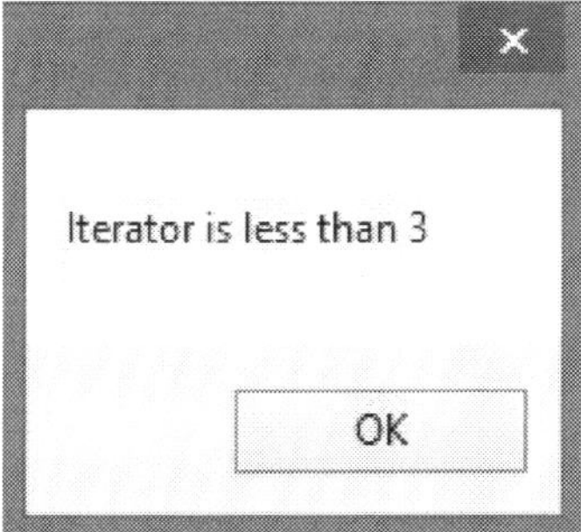

The loop has a condition with the Do Statement. Therefore, a decision must be made for the statement to be executed. In this case, i is set to one with the statement "i = 1." The condition "**Do Until** i < 3" will not execute because i, which equals one, is already less than three. The statement (**MsgBox** "Iterator = " & i) does not warrant an execution since the condition is True. The following is an example of the Do Until…Loop flowchart:

Figure 5.45

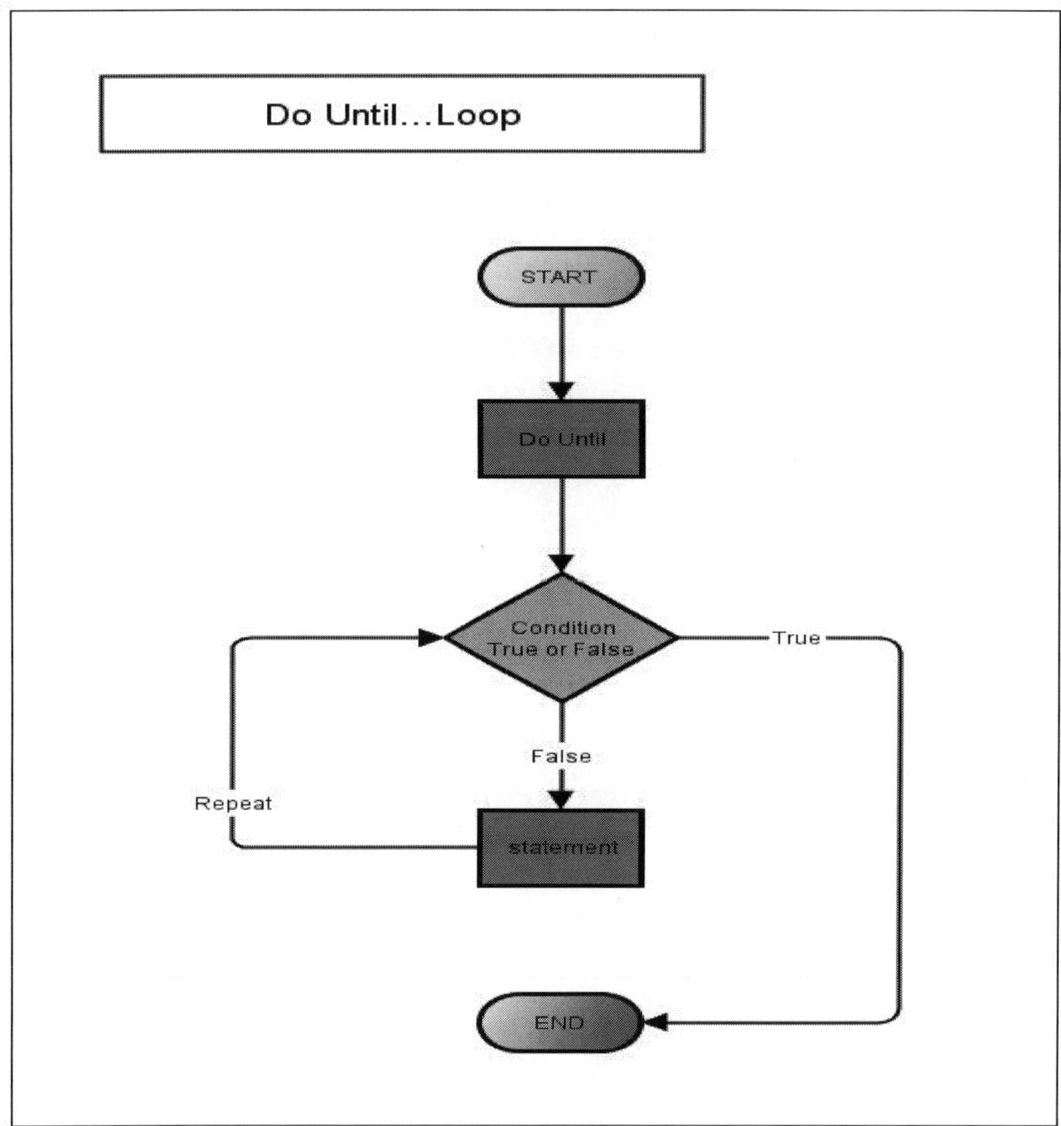

Skype: rex.jones34
Twitter: @RexJonesII
Email: Rex.Jones@Test4Success.org
LinkedIn: https://www.linkedin.com/in/rexjones34

Syntax

Do

<statement>

(Exit Do)

<statement>

Loop Until condition

Figure 5.46

```
Option Explicit
Dim i

i = 1

Do
        MsgBox "Iterator = " & i
        i = i + 1
Loop Until i < 3

MsgBox "Iterator is less than 3"
```

Option Explicit
Dim i

i = 1

Do
    MsgBox "Iterator = " & i
    i = i + 1
Loop Until i < 3

MsgBox "Iterator is less than 3"

3 Tips To Master QTP/UFT Within 30 Days
http://tinyurl.com/3-Tips-For-QTP-UFT

Free Webinars, Videos, and Live Trainings
http://tinyurl.com/Free-QTP-UFT-Selenium

The first output displays “Iterator = 1” and the second output displays “Iterator is less than 3”

Figure 5.47

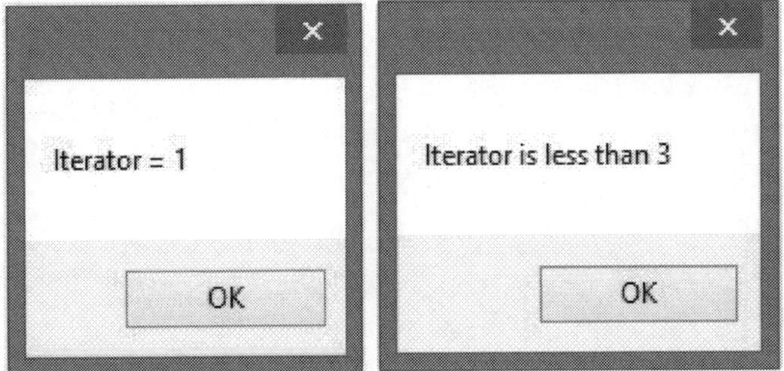

The statement is executed at least one time because there is not a condition on the Do Statement. The iterator equals one by setting “i = 1,” producing the first output (Iterator = 1) by way of the statement ”**MsgBox** "Iterator = " & i.” The iterator increases to two with the statement “i = i + 1.” The condition “**Loop Until** i < 3” causes the loop to stop because two is less than three, which displays the second output “Iterator is less than 3.” On the other hand, the statement “**MsgBox** (Iterator = " & i)” would have been repeated if the condition “**Loop Until** i < 3” is false. The following is an example of the Do…Loop Until flowchart:

Figure 5.48

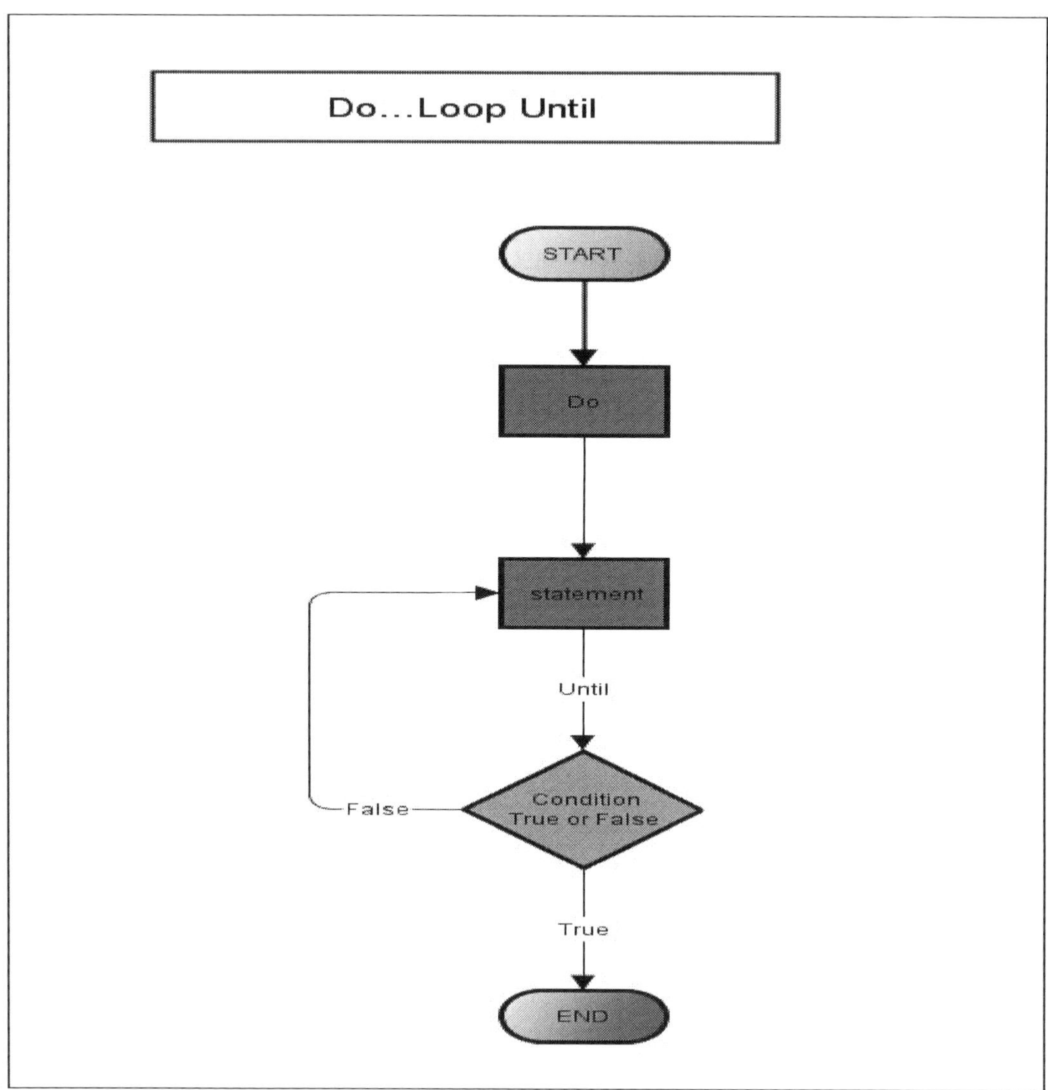
Do...Loop Until
START
Do
statement
Until
Condition
True or False
False
True
END

The advantage of the Do Loop is the versatility of using keywords While or Until and placing the keywords at the beginning or end of the loop. Generally, people choose one of the keywords for coding. An important question is whether the code should be executed at least once. If so, the condition will be placed at the end of the loop. If not, the condition will be placed at the beginning of the loop.

Chapter 5 explained the Flow Control by covering the Branching Constructs and Looping Statements. Chapter 6 will go into detail regarding Procedures and Functions.

Skype: rex.jones34
Twitter: @RexJonesII
Email: Rex.Jones@Test4Success.org
LinkedIn: https://www.linkedin.com/in/rexjones34

Chapter 6 Procedures—Functions

There are times when the terms procedures and functions are used interchangeably. For the sake of this chapter procedure will be the preferred term for sub and function, while function will be employed to reference Built-In Functions. Procedures allow programmers to modularize their code into named blocks of code that perform a specific task. Modularization describes complex code organized into modules, which increases the readability and clarity of the code. Modularization also creates an opportunity to reuse the same code. VBScript provides Built-In Functions for programmers, as well as permits programmers to write their own procedure (Sub and Function). Sub Procedure and Function Procedure involve three concepts:

1. **Named Block of Code**: Lines of code that are related in a logical manner and are used to perform a task. Procedures are called named blocks of code because they have a name with boundaries surrounding the code.
2. **Calling Code**: Code that calls a procedure. The main purpose of a procedure is to have a code call another block of code using a specific name.
3. **Values**: Some named blocks of code can return values to the calling code, while others cannot return values to the calling code. Sub Procedures do not return values but Function Procedures return values.

It is best for procedures to carry out a single action. The code can possibly become difficult to write and read if it has more than one task. The following are some good and bad task examples:

Good Examples

- Code that saves a file

- Code that adds numbers
- Code that processes a string

Bad Examples

- Code that processes a string, add numbers and saves a file
- Code that handles file access and database access
- Code that reads a file and writes to a file

Chapter six will cover:

- ✓ Sub Procedure
- ✓ Function Procedure
- ✓ Built-In Functions

Sub Procedure

A Sub Procedure is a named block of code enclosed by the code phrases Sub and End Sub, which perform an action, but do not return a value. Sub Procedures can optionally receive arguments such as constants, variables, or expressions from a calling code. In addition, programmers optionally precede the Sub keyword with keywords Public or Private to determine if the procedure is visible or not. The code keywords Public and Private are relevant only when dealing with classes. Public is the default, if Public or Private is not specified. The following is the syntax for a Sub Procedure:

Syntax
[Public | Private] Sub NameOfSubProcedure ([Argument1], [ArgumentN])
    code
End Sub

Figure 6.1

```
Option Explicit

Call GreetRex

Sub GreetRex
        MsgBox "Hi, Rex. Do you really offer a Reading Plan and Free Live Training?"
End Sub
```

Option Explicit

Call GreetRex

Sub GreetRex
    MsgBox "Hi, Rex. Do you really offer a Reading Plan and Free Live Training?"
End Sub

The output displays "Hi, Rex. Do you really offer a Reading Plan and Free Live Training?"

Figure 6.2

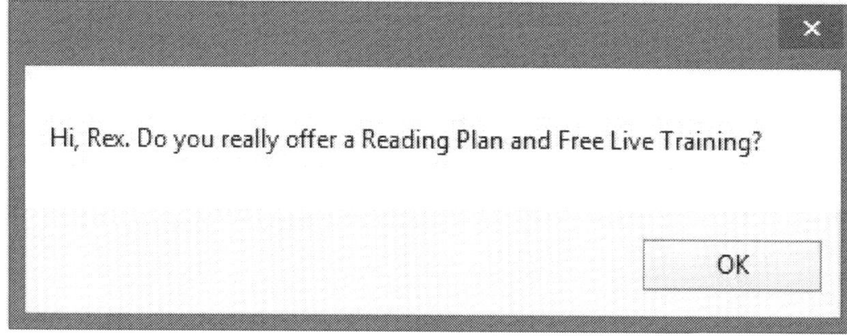

The first line "**Call** GreetRex" is the calling code that petitions the procedure. A procedure has no worth unless it is called by a code. Evaluate how keywords Public and Private, along with an argument after the procedure name, have been excluded. Adding an argument will make this procedure reusable. The following is an example of a procedure using one argument:

Figure 6.3

```
Option Explicit

Call GreetName("Rex")

Sub GreetName(strUserName)
    MsgBox "Hi, " & strUserName & "." & " Do you really offer a Reading Plan and Free Live Training?"
End Sub
```

Option Explicit

Call GreetName("Rex")

Sub GreetName(strUserName)
MsgBox "Hi, " & strUserName & "." & " Do you really offer a Reading Plan and Free Live Training?"
End Sub

The output displays "Hi, Rex. Do you really offer a Reading Plan and Free Live Training?"

Figure 6.4

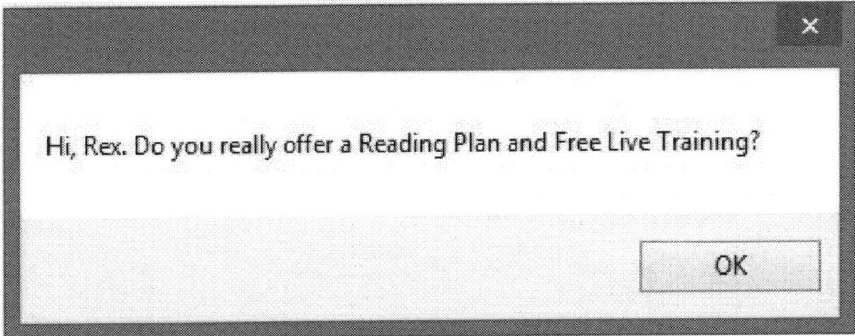

Imagine that a programmer wants to find the total of two numbers without using a procedure. The code would look like this:

Figure 6.5

```
Option Explicit
Dim intFirst, intSecond, intTotal

intFirst = 20
intSecond = 17

intTotal = intFirst + intSecond
MsgBox intTotal
```

Option Explicit
Dim intFirst, intSecond, intTotal

intFirst = 20
intSecond = 17

intTotal = intFirst + intSecond
MsgBox intTotal

The output displays "37" after adding "intFirst = 20" and "intSecond = 17."

Figure 6.6

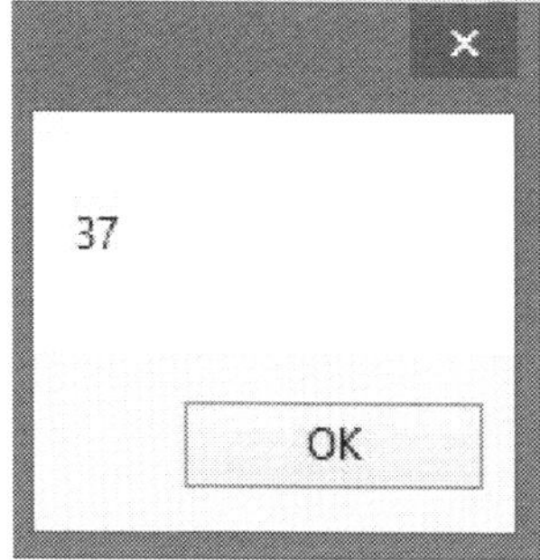

3 Tips To Master QTP/UFT Within 30 Days
http://tinyurl.com/3-Tips-For-QTP-UFT

Free Webinars, Videos, and Live Trainings
http://tinyurl.com/Free-QTP-UFT-Selenium

Suppose two more numbers are set to be added to the procedure for a new total. In this case, the previous code has to be repeated to show the output. The following is how the complete code looks with two additional numbers:

Figure 6.7

```
Option Explicit
Dim intFirst, intSecond, intThird, intFourth, intTotal

intFirst = 20
intSecond = 17

intTotal = intFirst + intSecond
MsgBox intTotal

intThird = 5
intFourth = 15

intTotal = intThird + intFourth
MsgBox intTotal
```

Option Explicit
Dim intFirst, intSecond, intThird, intFourth, intTotal

intFirst = 20
intSecond = 17

intTotal = intFirst + intSecond
MsgBox intTotal

intThird = 5
intFourth = 15

intTotal = intThird + intFourth
MsgBox intTotal

Skype: rex.jones34
Twitter: @RexJonesII
Email: Rex.Jones@Test4Success.org
LinkedIn: https://www.linkedin.com/in/rexjones34

The first output displays “37” and the second output displays “20.”

Figure 6.8

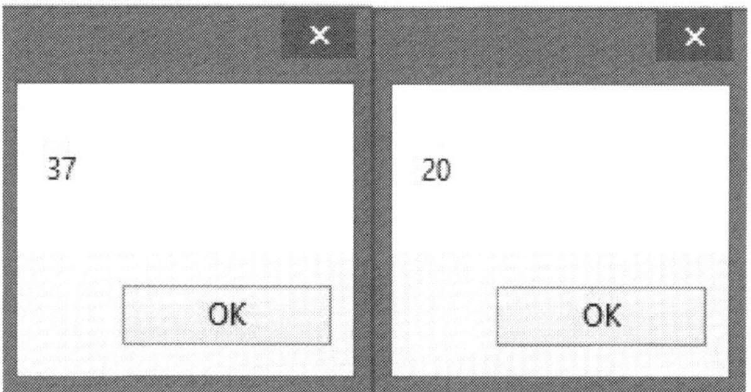

The above code requires high maintenance due to extra variables and more lines of code. The following is a Sub Procedure example that will produce the same results as above, but in a more efficient manner:

Figure 6.9

```
Option Explicit

Call AddNumbers (20, 17)
Call AddNumbers (5, 15)

Sub AddNumbers (intFirstNumber, intSecondNumber)
        MsgBox intFirstNumber + intSecondNumber
End Sub
```

Option Explicit

Call AddNumbers (20, 17)
Call AddNumbers (5, 15)

Sub AddNumbers (intFirstNumber, intSecondNumber)

3 Tips To Master QTP/UFT Within 30 Days
http://tinyurl.com/3-Tips-For-QTP-UFT

Free Webinars, Videos, and Live Trainings
http://tinyurl.com/Free-QTP-UFT-Selenium

MsgBox intFirstNumber + intSecondNumber
End Sub

The first output displays "37" and the second output displays "20."

Figure 6.10

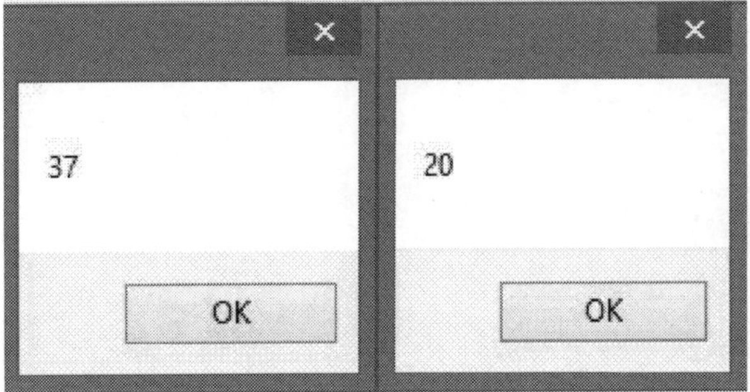

An error occurs if there is an attempt to return a value to the Sub Procedure. The following is an example that displays a Run Error:

Figure 6.11

```
Option Explicit

Dim intFirst, intSecond

intFirst = 20
intSecond = 17

MsgBox "This SubProcedure displays an error when attempting to return a value " & AddNumbers (intFirst, intSecond)

Sub AddNumbers (intFirstNumber, intSecondNumber)
        MsgBox "Sub Procedure does not return values. The first MsgBox displays a Run Error"
End Sub
```

Option Explicit

Dim intFirst, intSecond

intFirst = 20

intSecond = 17

MsgBox "This SubProcedure displays an error when attempting to return a value " & AddNumbers (intFirst, intSecond)

Sub AddNumbers (intFirstNumber, intSecondNumber)
    MsgBox "Sub Procedure does not return values. The first MsgBox displays a Run Error"
End Sub

A Run Error displays, "Type mismatch: AddNumbers" for Line 8.

Figure 6.12

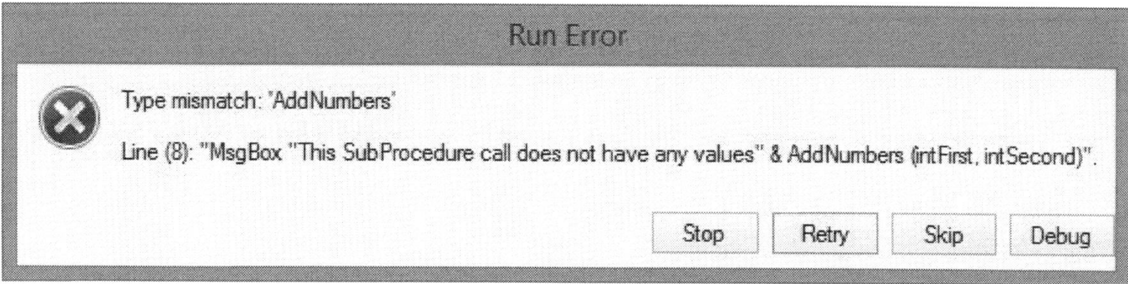

Function Procedure

A Function Procedure is a named block of code enclosed by Function and End Function, which perform an action and returns a value. The principles regarding keywords Public and Private and declaring arguments are identical to the Sub Procedure. The following is the syntax for a Function Procedure:

Syntax
[Public | Private] Function NameOfFunctionProcedure ([Argument1], [ArgumentN])
    code
    NameOfFunctionProcedure = some value

End Function

Figure 6.13

```
Option Explicit

Dim intFirst, intSecond

intFirst = 25
intSecond = 4

MsgBox "The total is " & MultiplyNumbers (intFirst, intSecond)

Function MultiplyNumbers (intFirstNumber, intSecondNumber)
        MultiplyNumbers = intFirstNumber * intSecondNumber
End Function
```

Option Explicit

Dim intFirst, intSecond

intFirst = 25
intSecond = 4

MsgBox "The total is " & MultiplyNumbers (intFirst, intSecond)

Function MultiplyNumbers (intFirstNumber, intSecondNumber)
    MultiplyNumbers = intFirstNumber * intSecondNumber
End Function

The output displays "The total is 100."

Figure 6.14

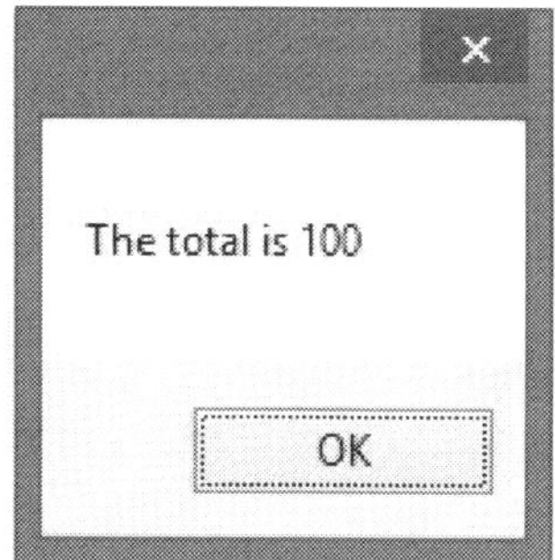

The Function Procedure has two arguments "intFirstNumber" and "intSecondNumber," which are named differently from the variables "intFirst" and "intSecond." Arguments and variables can have the same name, but this may cause confusion. Therefore, it is favorable to have unique names that are still similar enough to recognize the relationship between variables and arguments. Each argument provides a way for the code within the procedure to access values passed to it from the calling code. The following is a breakdown of the calling code and code within the procedure:

- Calling Code = **MsgBox** "The total is " & MultiplyNumbers (intFirst, intSecond)
- Code within the Procedure = (MultiplyNumbers = intFirstNumber * intSecondNumber)

The calling code variables pass values "25" and "4" to the procedure arguments. Variable intFirst passes 25 to argument intFirstNumber while intSecond passes 4 to argument intSecondNumber. Eventually the message box (MsgBox) displays the returned value "100" from the procedure. Notice the code within the procedure. The function name "MultiplyNumbers" and arguments intFirstNumber and intSecondNumber are not explicitly declared with a Dim statement. An explicit declaration is not required by virtue of statement "**Function** MultiplyNumbers (intFirstNumber, intSecondNumber)," which implicitly declares the function name and arguments. However, the program would have encountered an error if the procedure used an undeclared variable (i.e. intTotal). Function Procedures can only return values if the value is stored inside the function name. As a result, "intFirstNumber = 25" multiplied by "intSecondNumber = 4" assigns 100 to function name MultiplyNumbers, which returns 100 back to the calling code.

Procedure Techniques/Rules

It is beneficial to use meaningful procedure names that make the purpose clear. A good technique to employ is verb-noun combinations, such as "GetOrder." Programmers can use as many arguments as needed, although a sign of a procedure with too many tasks is too many arguments. The same rules that apply to naming a procedure apply to naming variables:

1. Cannot exceed 255 characters
2. Underscore "_" is the only valid non-alphanumeric character
3. Must start with a letter (uppercase or lowercase)

Syntax for Calling Procedures

There are several methods to invoke a Sub Procedure or Function Procedure. This section illustrates valid and invalid ways for calling Sub and Function Procedures.

Call Sub Procedure

The Call keyword requires a parenthesis when calling a Sub Procedure. Conversely, the parenthesis can be used with the Call keyword or without the Call keyword.

Valid

Syntax

NameOfSubProcedure "some value"

Figure 6.15

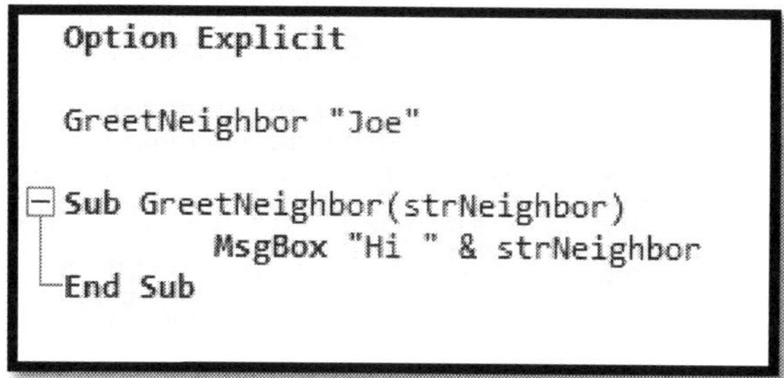

```
Option Explicit

GreetNeighbor "Joe"

Sub GreetNeighbor(strNeighbor)
      MsgBox "Hi " & strNeighbor
End Sub
```

The output displays "Hi Joe."

Figure 6.16

3 Tips To Master QTP/UFT Within 30 Days
http://tinyurl.com/3-Tips-For-QTP-UFT

Free Webinars, Videos, and Live Trainings
http://tinyurl.com/Free-QTP-UFT-Selenium

Syntax

Call NameOfSubProcedure ("some value")

Figure 6.17

```
Option Explicit

Call GreetNeighbor ("Joe")

Sub GreetNeighbor(strNeighbor)
        MsgBox "Hi " & strNeighbor
End Sub
```

Option Explicit

Call GreetNeighbor ("Joe")

Sub GreetNeighbor(strNeighbor)
    MsgBox "Hi " & strNeighbor
End Sub

The output displays “Hi Joe.”

Figure 6.18

Skype: rex.jones34
Twitter: @RexJonesII
Email: Rex.Jones@Test4Success.org
LinkedIn: https://www.linkedin.com/in/rexjones34

Syntax

NameOfSubProcedure ("some value")

Figure 6.19

```
Option Explicit

GreetNeighbor ("Joe")

Sub GreetNeighbor(strNeighbor)
        MsgBox "Hi " & strNeighbor
End Sub
```

Option Explicit

GreetNeighbor ("Joe")

Sub GreetNeighbor(strNeighbor)
    MsgBox "Hi " & strNeighbor
End Sub

The output displays "Hi Joe."

Figure 6.20

3 Tips To Master QTP/UFT Within 30 Days
http://tinyurl.com/3-Tips-For-QTP-UFT

Free Webinars, Videos, and Live Trainings
http://tinyurl.com/Free-QTP-UFT-Selenium

Invalid

Syntax

Call NameOfSubProcedure "some value"

Figure 6.21

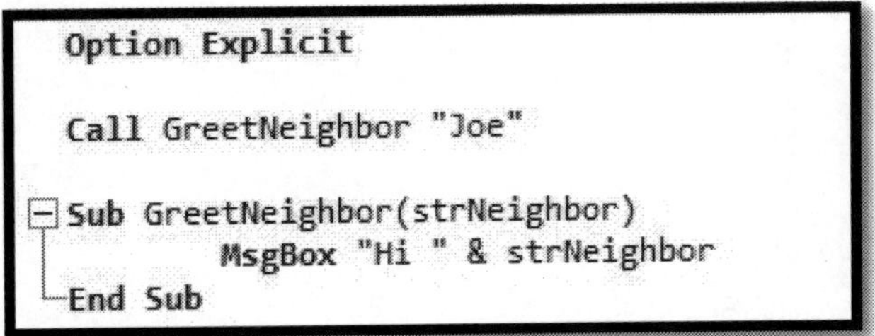

```
Option Explicit

Call GreetNeighbor "Joe"

Sub GreetNeighbor(strNeighbor)
    MsgBox "Hi " & strNeighbor
End Sub
```

A Run Error displays “The test run cannot continue due to a syntax error.”

Skype: rex.jones34
Twitter: @RexJonesII
Email: Rex.Jones@Test4Success.org
LinkedIn: https://www.linkedin.com/in/rexjones34

Figure 6.22

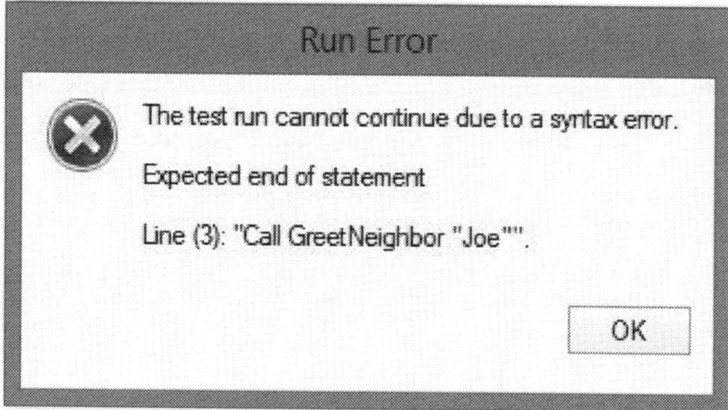

Call Function Procedure

The rules for calling a Function Procedure are different. Parenthesis must surround the argument list and the Call keyword has to be omitted to receive a value from the function.

Valid

Syntax

MsgBox NameOfFunctionProcedure (some value)

Figure 6.23

```
Option Explicit

MsgBox AddNumbers (1, 2, 3)

Function AddNumbers (intFirstNumber, intSecondNumber, intThirdNumber)
        AddNumbers = intFirstNumber + intSecondNumber + intThirdNumber
End Function
```

```
Option Explicit

MsgBox AddNumbers (1, 2, 3)

Function AddNumbers (intFirstNumber, intSecondNumber, intThirdNumber)
    AddNumbers = intFirstNumber + intSecondNumber + intThirdNumber
End Function
```

The output displays "6."

Figure 6.24

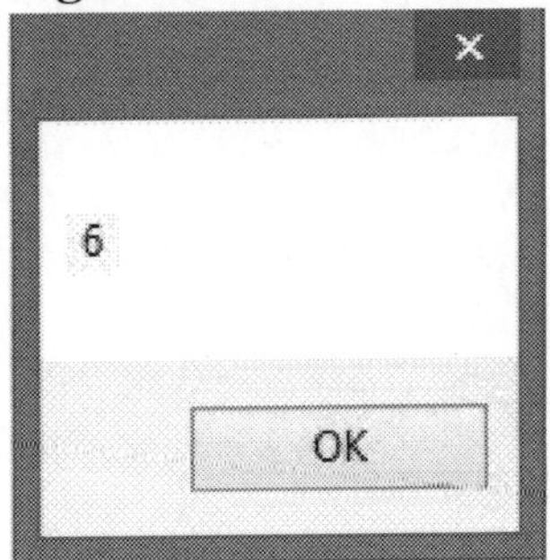

Syntax
variable = NameOfFunctionProcedure (some value)

Figure 6.25

```
Option Explicit
Dim intTotal

intTotal = AddNumbers (1, 2, 3)
MsgBox intTotal

Function AddNumbers (intFirstNumber, intSecondNumber, intThirdNumber)
        AddNumbers = intFirstNumber + intSecondNumber + intThirdNumber
End Function
```

Option Explicit
Dim intTotal

intTotal = AddNumbers (1, 2, 3)
MsgBox intTotal

Function AddNumbers (intFirstNumber, intSecondNumber, intThirdNumber)
    AddNumbers = intFirstNumber + intSecondNumber + intThirdNumber
End Function

The output displays "6."

Figure 6.26

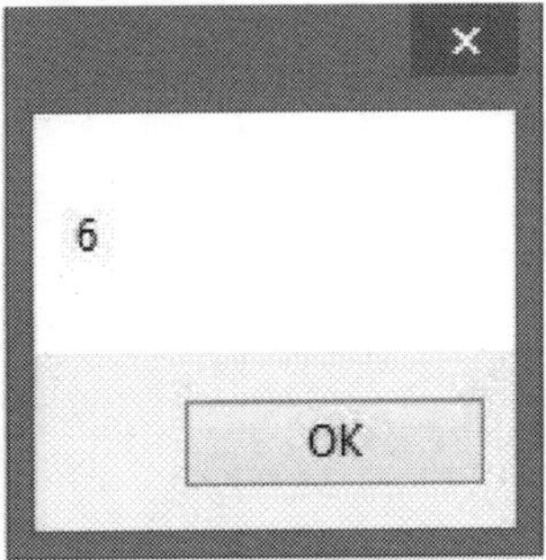

Invalid

Syntax

variable = NameOfFunctionProcedure some value

Figure 6.27

```
Option Explicit
Dim intTotal

intTotal = AddNumbers 1, 2, 3
MsgBox intTotal

Function AddNumbers (intFirstNumber, intSecondNumber, intThirdNumber)
        AddNumbers = intFirstNumber + intSecondNumber + intThirdNumber
End Function
```

Option Explicit
Dim intTotal

intTotal = AddNumbers 1, 2, 3
MsgBox intTotal

```
Function AddNumbers (intFirstNumber, intSecondNumber, intThirdNumber)
    AddNumbers = intFirstNumber + intSecondNumber + intThirdNumber
End Function
```

A Run Error displays "The test run cannot continue due to a syntax error."

Figure 6.28

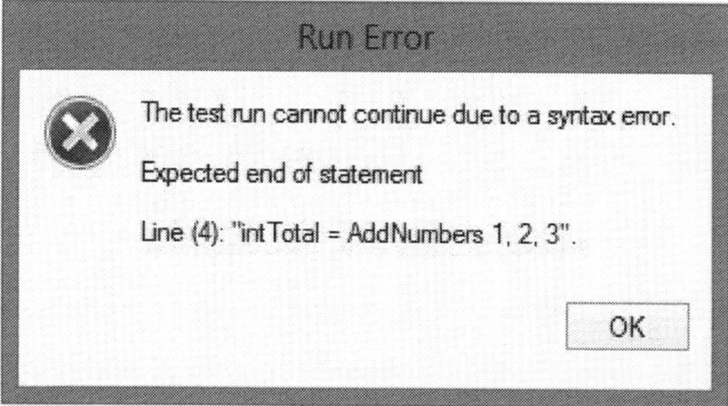

Syntax

variable = Call NameOfFunctionProcedure some value

Figure 6.29

```
Option Explicit
Dim intTotal

intTotal = Call AddNumbers (1, 2, 3)
MsgBox intTotal

Function AddNumbers (intFirstNumber, intSecondNumber, intThirdNumber)
        AddNumbers = intFirstNumber + intSecondNumber + intThirdNumber
End Function
```

3 Tips To Master QTP/UFT Within 30 Days
http://tinyurl.com/3-Tips-For-QTP-UFT

Free Webinars, Videos, and Live Trainings
http://tinyurl.com/Free-QTP-UFT-Selenium

```
Option Explicit
Dim intTotal

intTotal = Call AddNumbers (1, 2, 3)
MsgBox intTotal

Function AddNumbers (intFirstNumber, intSecondNumber, intThirdNumber)
    AddNumbers = intFirstNumber + intSecondNumber + intThirdNumber
End Function
```

A Run Error displays "The test run cannot continue due to a syntax error."

Figure 6.30

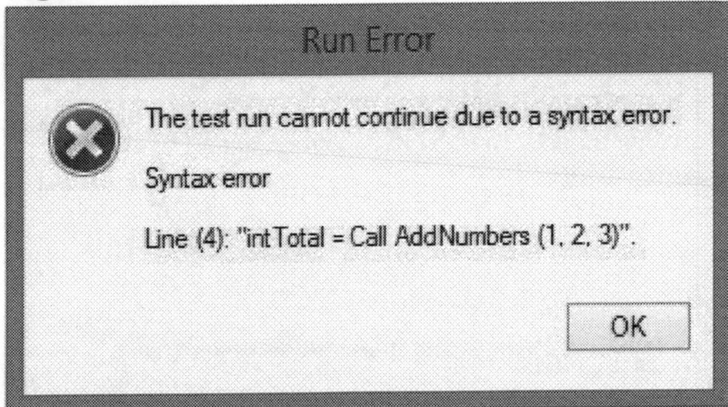

Argument Declaration (ByRef or ByVal)

An argument is represented by reference (ByRef) or by value (ByVal), according to how it is declared in the procedure. ByRef is the default if there is not a declaration. A change to the value in a procedure is permanent and reflected in the calling code when using ByRef. On the contrary, designating an argument as ByVal means that the code within a procedure can change the value of a variable, but they are not permanent. The changes are eliminated as soon as the procedure terminates. The following is an example of not declaring the arguments using ByRef and ByVal:

Figure 6.31

```
Option Explicit
Dim intFirst, intSecond

intFirst = 100
intSecond = 100

Call No_ByRef_ByVal (intFirst, intSecond)
MsgBox "intFirst = " & intFirst & vbNewLine & "intSecond = " & intSecond

Sub No_ByRef_ByVal (intFirstNumber, intSecondNumber)

        intFirstNumber = intFirstNumber + 10
        intSecondNumber = intSecondNumber + 10

        MsgBox "intFirstNumber = " & intFirstNumber & vbNewLine & _
        "intSecondNumber = " & intSecondNumber

End Sub
```

Option Explicit
Dim intFirst, intSecond

intFirst = 100
intSecond = 100

Call No_ByRef_ByVal (intFirst, intSecond)
MsgBox "intFirst = " & intFirst & **vbNewLine** & "intSecond = " & intSecond

Sub No_ByRef_ByVal (intFirstNumber, intSecondNumber)

    intFirstNumber = intFirstNumber + 10

```
    intSecondNumber = intSecondNumber + 10

    MsgBox "intFirstNumber = " & intFirstNumber & vbNewLine & _
    "intSecondNumber = " & intSecondNumber

End Sub
```

The first output displays "intFirstNumber = 110" and "intSecondNumber = 110" while the second output displays "intFirst = 110" and "intSecond = 110."

Figure 6.32

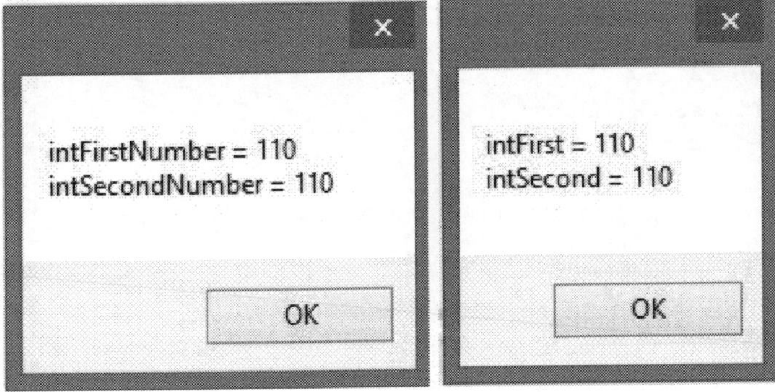

The following is an example of declaring the arguments using ByRef and ByVal:

Figure 6.33

```
Option Explicit
Dim intFirst, intSecond

intFirst = 100
intSecond = 100

Call ByRef_ByVal (intFirst, intSecond)
MsgBox "intFirst = " & intFirst & vbNewLine & "intSecond = " & intSecond

Sub ByRef_ByVal (ByRef intFirstNumber, ByVal intSecondNumber)

        intFirstNumber = intFirstNumber + 10
        intSecondNumber = intSecondNumber + 10

        MsgBox "intFirstNumber = " & intFirstNumber & vbNewLine & _
        "intSecondNumber = " & intSecondNumber

End Sub
```

Option Explicit
Dim intFirst, intSecond

intFirst = 100
intSecond = 100

Call ByRef_ByVal (intFirst, intSecond)
MsgBox "intFirst = " & intFirst & **vbNewLine** & "intSecond = " & intSecond

Sub ByRef_ByVal (**ByRef** intFirstNumber, **ByVal** intSecondNumber)

intFirstNumber = intFirstNumber + 10
intSecondNumber = intSecondNumber + 10

3 Tips To Master QTP/UFT Within 30 Days
http://tinyurl.com/3-Tips-For-QTP-UFT

Free Webinars, Videos, and Live Trainings
http://tinyurl.com/Free-QTP-UFT-Selenium

```
    MsgBox "intFirstNumber = " & intFirstNumber & vbNewLine & _
    "intSecondNumber = " & intSecondNumber

End Sub
```

The first output displays "intFirstNumber = 110" and "intSecondNumber = 110," while the second output displays "intFirst = 110" and "intSecond = 100."

Figure 6.34

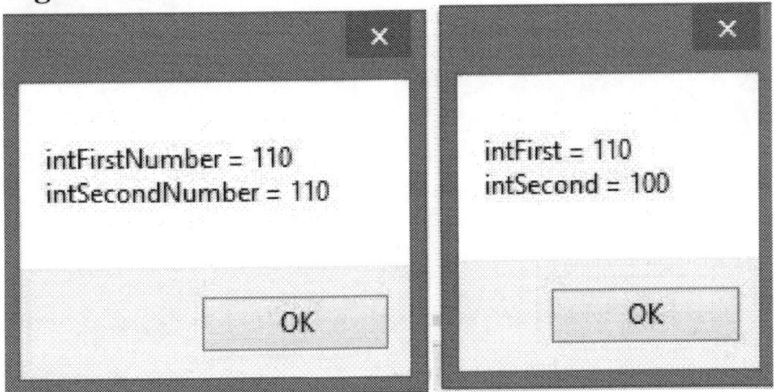

The variables intFirst and intSecond are declared at the script level and initialized to 100. Argument intFirstNumber is declared as ByRef and argument intSecondNumber as ByVal. Both arguments are increased by ten within the procedure "ByRef_ByVal," which outputs "110" (Figure 6.32 "1st dialog"). Observe how intFirst has a value of 110 (Figure 6.32 "2nd dialog"). Only intFirst was changed outside of the procedure because it was passed by reference. Variable intSecond was passed by value and displays 100 (Figure 6.32 "2nd dialog"). ByRef value changes are not reflected outside of the procedure.

Built-In Functions

VBScript automatically provides a library of functions called Built-In Functions. The Built-In Functions allow programmers to be more efficient and not waste time creating a function that already exists. MsgBox is a Built-In Function with several parameters that have been used throughout this book. The first parameter displays a message in a dialog box while the other parameters, such as the button parameter (second parameter) and title parameter (third parameter), are optional. The following is a MsgBox example using the button and title parameters:

Option Explicit

MsgBox "Do you want to join Rex Jones for Free Live Training? ", **VbYesNo**, "FREE LIVE TRAINING"

The output displays "Do you want to join Rex Jones for Free Live Training?"

Figure 6.35

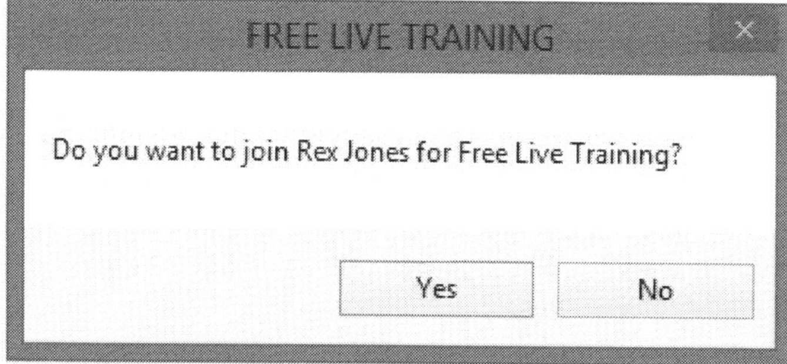

Normally, the dialog displays a message and an OK button. This example shows a title "FREE LIVE TRAINING," a message "Do you want to join Rex Jones for Free Live Training," and two buttons Yes and No. In most cases, programmers only use the MsgBox function for debugging purposes. Therefore, the optional parameters are not necessary. The following is a list of some useful Built-In Functions divided by the following sections:

- Array Functions
- Conversion Functions
- Date/Time Functions
- Format Functions

3 Tips To Master QTP/UFT Within 30 Days
http://tinyurl.com/3-Tips-For-QTP-UFT

Free Webinars, Videos, and Live Trainings
http://tinyurl.com/Free-QTP-UFT-Selenium

- Math Functions
- Miscellaneous Functions
- String Functions

Array Functions

Figure 6.36

Function	Description
Array	Returns a variant containing an array
Filter	Returns a zero-based array that contains a subset of a string array based on a filter criteria
IsArray	Returns a Boolean value that indicates whether a specified variable is an array
Join	Returns a string that consists of a number of substrings in an array
LBound	Returns the smallest subscript for the indicated dimension of an array
Split	Returns a zero-based, one-dimensional array that contains a specified number of substrings
UBound	Returns the largest subscript for the indicated dimension of an array

Conversion Functions

Figure 6.37

Function	Description
Asc	Converts the first letter in a string to American National Standards Institute (ANSI) code
CBool	Converts an expression to a variant of subtype Boolean
CByte	Converts an expression to a variant of subtype Byte
CCur	Converts an expression to a variant of subtype Currency
CDate	Converts a valid date and time expression to the variant of subtype Date

CDbl	Converts an expression to a variant of subtype Double
Chr	Converts the specified ANSI code to a character
CInt	Converts an expression to a variant of subtype Integer
CLng	Converts an expression to a variant of subtype Long
CSng	Converts an expression to a variant of subtype Single
CStr	Converts an expression to a variant of subtype String

Date / Time Functions

Figure 6.38

Function	Description
Date	Returns the current system date
DateAdd	Returns a date to which a specified time interval has been added
DateDiff	Returns the number of intervals between two dates
DatePart	Returns the specified part of a given date
DateSerial	Returns the date for a specified year, month, and day
DateValue	Returns a date
Day	Returns a number that represents the day of the month (between 1 and 31, inclusive)
FormatDateTime	Returns an expression formatted as a date or time
Hour	Returns a number that represents the hour of the day (between 0 and 23, inclusive)
IsDate	Returns a Boolean value that indicates if the evaluated expression can be converted to a date
Minute	Returns a number that represents the minute of the hour (between 0 and 59, inclusive)
Month	Returns a number that represents the month of the year (between 1 and 12, inclusive)
MonthName	Returns the name of a specified month
Now	Returns the current system date and time

3 Tips To Master QTP/UFT Within 30 Days
http://tinyurl.com/3-Tips-For-QTP-UFT

Free Webinars, Videos, and Live Trainings
http://tinyurl.com/Free-QTP-UFT-Selenium

Second	Returns a number that represents the second of the minute (between 0 and 59, inclusive)
Time	Returns the current system time
Timer	Returns the number of seconds since 12:00 AM
TimeSerial	Returns the time for a specific hour, minute, and second
TimeValue	Returns a time
Weekday	Returns a number that represents the day of the week (between 1 and 7, inclusive)
WeekdayName	Returns the weekday name of a specified day of the week
Year	Returns a number that represents the year

Format Functions

Figure 6.39

Function	Description
FormatCurrency	Returns an expression formatted as a currency value
FormatNumber	Returns an expression formatted as a number
FormatPercent	Returns an expression formatted as a percentage

Math Functions

Figure 6.40

Function	Description
Abs	Returns the absolute value of a specified number
Atn	Returns the arctangent of a specified number. The Atn function takes the ratio of two sides of a right triangle and returns the corresponding angle in radians. The ratio is the length of the side opposite the angle divided by the length of the side adjacent to the angle.
Cos	Returns the cosine of a specified number (angle). The Cos function takes an angle and returns the ratio of two sides of a

	right triangle. The ratio is the length of the side adjacent to the angle divided by the length of the hypotenuse.
Exp	Returns "*e*" raised to a power
Hex	Returns the hexadecimal value of a specified number
Int	Returns the integer part of a specified number. If a number is negative, the Int function returns the first negative integer less than or equal to the number
Fix	Returns the integer part of a specified number. If a number is negative, then the Fix function returns the first negative integer greater than or equal to the number
Log	Returns the natural logarithm of a specified number. The natural logarithm is the logarithm to the base *e*. The constant *e* is approximately 2.718282.
Oct	Returns the octal value of a specified number. Octal is the base-8 number system which uses the digits 0 to 7.
Rnd	Returns a random number less than 1 but greater or equal to 0
Sgn	Returns an integer that indicates the sign of a specified number
Sin	Returns the sine of a specified number (angle). The Sin function takes an angle and returns the ratio of two sides of a right triangle. The ratio is the length of the side opposite the angle divided by the length of the hypotenuse.
Sqr	Returns the square root of a specified number
Tan	Returns the tangent of a specified number (angle). The Tan function takes an angle and returns the ratio of two sides of a right triangle. The ratio is the length of the side opposite the angle divided by the length of the side adjacent to the angle.

Miscellaneous Functions

Figure 6.41

Function	Description
CreateObject	Creates an object of a specified type

3 Tips To Master QTP/UFT Within 30 Days
http://tinyurl.com/3-Tips-For-QTP-UFT

Free Webinars, Videos, and Live Trainings
http://tinyurl.com/Free-QTP-UFT-Selenium

Eval	Evaluates an expression and returns the result
InputBox	Displays a prompt in a dialog box, waits for the user to input text or click a button, and returns the contents of the text box
IsEmpty	Returns a Boolean value that indicates whether a specified variable has been initialized or not
IsNothing	Used to test if a value is an initialized object
IsNull	Returns a Boolean value that indicates whether a specified expression contains no valid data (Null)
IsNumeric	Returns a Boolean value that indicates whether a specified expression can be evaluated as a number
IsObject	Returns a Boolean value that indicates whether the specified expression is an automation object
LoadPicture	Returns a picture object
MsgBox	Returns a message
RGB	Returns a number that represents an RGB color value
Round	Rounds a number
ScriptEngine	Returns the scripting language in use
ScriptEngineBuildVersion	Returns the build version number of the scripting engine in use
ScriptEngineMajorVersion	Returns the major version number of the scripting engine in use
ScriptEngineMinorVersion	Returns the minor version number of the scripting engine in use
TypeName	Returns the subtype of a specified variable
VarType	Returns a value that indicates the subtype of a specified variable

String Functions

Figure 6.42

Function	Description

InStr	Returns the position of the first occurrence of one string within another. The search begins at the first character of the string
InStrRev	Returns the position of the first occurrence of one string within another. The search begins at the last character of the string
LCase	Converts a specified string to lowercase
Left	Returns a specified number of characters from the left side of a string
Len	Returns the number of characters in a string
LTrim	Removes spaces on the left side of a string
RTrim	Removes spaces on the right side of a string
Trim	Removes spaces on both the left and the right side of a string
Mid	Returns a specified number of characters from a string
Replace	Replaces a specified part of a string with another string a specified number of times
Right	Returns a specified number of characters from the right side of a string
Space	Returns a string that consists of a specified number of spaces
StrComp	Compares two strings and returns a value that represents the result of the comparison
String	Returns a string that contains a repeating character of a specified length
StrReverse	Reverses a string
UCase	Converts a specified string to uppercase

Chapter 6 discussed procedures and functions. The two procedures are Sub Procedure and Function Procedure. Function Procedures return values while Sub Procedures do not return values. There are several functions called Built-In Functions that allow programmers to be efficient with their code. Chapter 7 describes the concept of creating and destroying objects.

3 Tips To Master QTP/UFT Within 30 Days
http://tinyurl.com/3-Tips-For-QTP-UFT

Free Webinars, Videos, and Live Trainings
http://tinyurl.com/Free-QTP-UFT-Selenium

Chapter 7
Create and Destroy Objects

Objects are different from other Sub Data Types because they need to be created explicitly with a separate command. Like variables, objects have a location in the computer's memory, but the object's variable only holds a reference to the object. In other words, the object's variable contain information (also known as an address) for locating the object in memory.

Chapter seven will cover the following principles of objects:

- ✓ Create Objects
- ✓ Properties and Methods
- ✓ Multiple References
- ✓ With Construct
- ✓ Destroy Objects

Note: All of the examples in this chapter use a Dictionary Object *(see Dictionary Objects in Chapter 2 "Part 2 - You Must Learn VBScript for QTP – UFT".)*

Create Objects

Before using objects, an instance of the object must be created with its reference stored in a variable. The creation of an object is also known as instantiating an object. A copy of the object is assigned to the code that created the object. The following is the syntax for creating an object using a Dictionary Object:

Syntax
CreateObject(Servername.**Typename**[, Location])

Figure 7.1

Parameter	Description
Servername	Required. The name of the application that provides the object
Typename	Required. The type/class of the object
Location	Optional. Where to create the object

Figure 7.2

```
Option Explicit
Dim objGreet

Set objGreet = CreateObject("Scripting.Dictionary")

objGreet.Add 1, "James"

MsgBox "How many objects are in objGreet: " & objGreet.Count
```

Option Explicit
Dim objGreet

Set objGreet = **CreateObject(**"Scripting.Dictionary")

objGreet.Add 1, "James"

MsgBox "How many objects are in objGreet: " & objGreet.Count

The output displays "How many objects are in objGreet: 1."

Figure 7.3

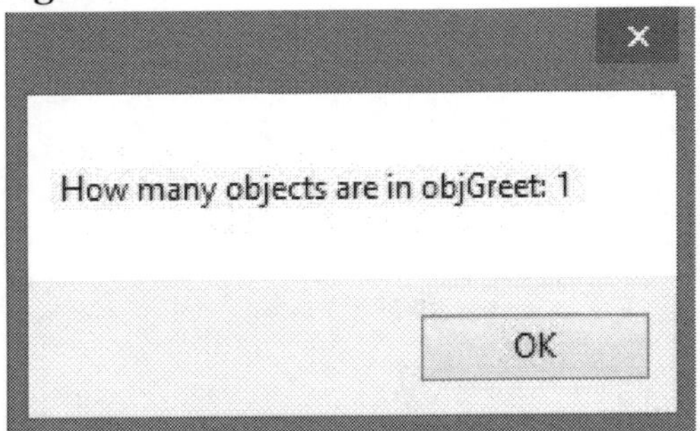

The code declares a variable to reserve the object: "objGreet," then uses the Set command and CreateObject function to create the object. Set commands are used when an object variable must be initialized. At the same time, the CreateObject function has the assignment of creating the object once the object name "Scripting.Dictionary" is passed. After the Add method: "objGreet.Add" adds an item pair, the MsgBox displays "1" because it is the value of the object's Count property: "objGreet.Count."

Properties and Methods

Objects can be accessed using properties and methods. A property is a placeholder for a value associated with a specific object. Properties can hold any kind of data, including a reference to another object. A method is comparable to a procedure that is attached to an object. Methods carry out a specific action for an object in the same manner as a procedure.

Multiple References

The value of an object's variable is a reference and not the object itself. This concept is important when programmers are dealing with multiple references to the same object. There are times when understanding an object's variable referencing an object can be confusing. In a brief form, an object's variable and object is similar to a person with a house. The person has a house wherefore the address identifies where the person dwells. An object's variable holds information that shows where the object dwells in a computer's memory. Regarding this section, multiple references to the same object is similar to one person having multiple houses. The following is an example of multiple object variables referencing the same object:

Figure 7.4

```
Option Explicit
Dim objGreet, objName
Dim strGreet, strName

Set objGreet = CreateObject("Scripting.Dictionary")
Set objName = objGreet

'Add and Display the item for objGreet
objGreet.Add "1", "James"
strGreet = objGreet.Item("1")
MsgBox "(objGreet) = " & strGreet

'Update and Display the item for objName
objName.Item("1") = "Joe"
strName = objName.Item("1")
MsgBox "(objName) = " & strName

'Display the item for objGreet after updating objName
strGreet = objGreet.Item("1")
MsgBox "(objGreet) = " & strGreet
```

Option Explicit
Dim objGreet, objName
Dim strGreet, strName

Set objGreet = **CreateObject**("Scripting.Dictionary")
Set objName = objGreet

3 Tips To Master QTP/UFT Within 30 Days
http://tinyurl.com/3-Tips-For-QTP-UFT

Free Webinars, Videos, and Live Trainings
http://tinyurl.com/Free-QTP-UFT-Selenium

```
'Add and Display the item for objGreet
objGreet.Add "1", "James"
strGreet = objGreet.Item("1")
MsgBox "(objGreet) = " & strGreet

'Update and Display the item for objName
objName.Item("1") = "Joe"
strName = objName.Item("1")
MsgBox "(objName) = " & strName

'Display the item for objGreet after updating objName
strGreet = objGreet.Item("1")
MsgBox "(objGreet) = " & strGreet
```

The first output displays "(objGreet) = James," the second output displays "(objName) = Joe," and the third output displays "(objGreet) = Joe."

Figure 7.5

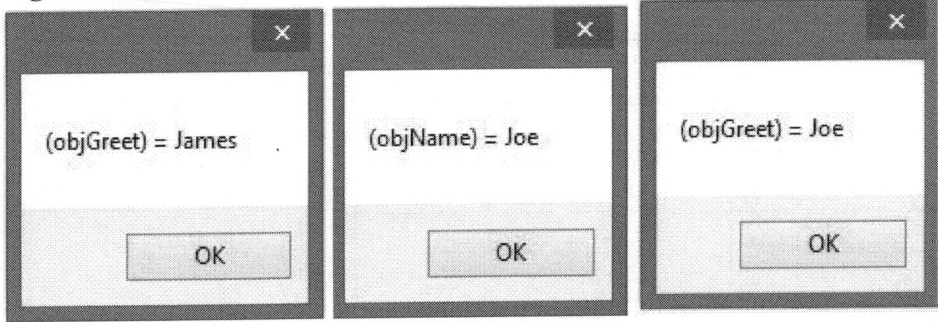

There are two object variables: "objGreet" and "objName" that are created by separate statements. Object variable objGreet was created by the Set command and the CreateObject function, but object variable objName was only created by the Set command. The line "**Set** objName = objGreet" means both variables are referencing the same object. Either object variable can update the object even though there is one Add method:

"objGreet.Add "1", "James"" on "objGreet". In this situation, "objName" updates the object with line "objName.Item("1") = "Joe"" which is reflected in both variables. Notice how "**MsgBox** "(objName) = " & strName" and "**MsgBox** "(objGreet) = " & strGreet" both display Joe.

With Construct

The With Construct is a shortcut that saves typing when referring to the same object more than once. The With Construct makes the programmer's code look clean when there are several lines of code. The With Construct requires statements to be enclosed within the "With…End With" block. The following is an example of the With Construct:

Figure 7.6

```
Option Explicit
Dim objGreet
Dim strGreet

Set objGreet = CreateObject("Scripting.Dictionary")

With objGreet
        .Add 1, "James"
        MsgBox "The count is " & .Count

        strGreet = .Item(1)
        MsgBox "Hello " & strGreet
End With
```

Option Explicit
Dim objGreet
Dim strGreet

Set objGreet = **CreateObject**("Scripting.Dictionary")

3 Tips To Master QTP/UFT Within 30 Days
http://tinyurl.com/3-Tips-For-QTP-UFT

Free Webinars, Videos, and Live Trainings
http://tinyurl.com/Free-QTP-UFT-Selenium

```
With objGreet
    .Add 1, "James"
    MsgBox "The count is " & .Count

    strGreet = .Item(1)
    MsgBox "Hello " & strGreet
End With
```

The first output displays "The count is 1" and the second output displays "Hello James."

Figure 7.7

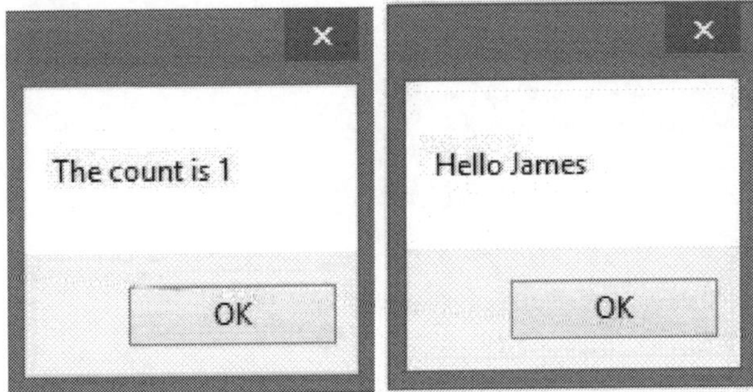

In the With…End With block of code object variable objGreet contains the Add method: ".Add 1, "James"," the Count property: ".Count," and the Item property: ".Item(1)," without typing the object variable each time.

Destroy Objects

Objects consume a large amount of resources. It is important to create objects before they are put to use and to also destroy objects when they are not needed. The key to understanding objects is recognizing their lifetime. An object remains in memory as long as a variable refers to the object. The object can lose its reference in one of two ways: First, the object variable can go out of scope and second, the object can be cleared out by using the keyword Nothing.

Nothing is a special value that is only used with objects to empty the reference. The following is an example using the keyword Nothing:

Figure 7.8

```
Option Explicit
Dim objGreet

Set objGreet = CreateObject("Scripting.Dictionary")

objGreet.Add "Greet", "Hello"

MsgBox "How many objects are in objGreet: " & objGreet.Count

Set objGreet = Nothing
```

Option Explicit
Dim objGreet

Set objGreet = **CreateObject**("Scripting.Dictionary")

objGreet.Add "Greet", "Hello"

MsgBox "How many objects are in objGreet: " & objGreet.Count

Set objGreet = Nothing

In this example, the object "objGreet" is cleared from memory by using the keyword Nothing.

Conclusion

VBScript is the scripting language that supports QTP/UFT scripts. An understanding of VBScript helps to create and maintain test scripts in QTP/UFT. This book: "Part 1—You Must Learn VBScript for QTP/UFT" focused on providing automation engineers a good foundation of the scripting language. Some of the take-away topics are:

Coding Standards: Automation engineers must implement good programming habits, such as comments and the Hungarian Naming Convention for variables.

Flow Control: Branching constructs and looping statements are two forms of flow control, which is the order of executing test scripts.

Sub Procedures: A way to modularize a block of code to perform an action without returning a value.

Function Procedures: A way to modularize a block of code to perform an action and return a value.

The second VBScript book is called "Part 2—You Must Learn VBScript for QTP/UFT." The second book dives into Dictionary Objects, FileSystemObject (FSO), Classes, Regular Expressions, Windows Script Host (WSH), Windows Management Instrumentation (WMI), Debugging and Handling Errors.

Skype: rex.jones34
Twitter: @RexJonesII
Email: Rex.Jones@Test4Success.org
LinkedIn: https://www.linkedin.com/in/rexjones34

Download PDF Version

The PDF Version of this book is available to you at the following link.

http://tinyurl.com/Part-1-VBScript-4-QTP-UFT

If the book was helpful, can you leave a favorable review?

http://tinyurl.com/Review-Part-1-VBScript-4-QTP

Thanks in advance,

Rex Allen Jones II

Books by Rex Jones II

1. **Free Book** Absolute Beginner
   (Part 1) You Must Learn VBScript for QTP/UFT
   Don't Ignore The Language For Functional Automation Testing

2. (Part 2) You Must Learn VBScript for QTP/UFT
   Don't Ignore The Language For Functional Automation Testing

3. **Free Book** Absolute Beginner
   (Part 1) Java 4 Selenium WebDriver
   Come Learn How To Program For Automation Testing

4. (Part 2) Java 4 Selenium WebDriver
   Come Learn How To Program For Automation Testing

Coming Soon

5. **Free Book** Absolute Beginner
   (Part 1) Selenium WebDriver for Functional Automation Testing
   Your Beginners Guide To Become Good

6. (Part 2) Selenium WebDriver for Functional Automation Testing
   Your Guide To Stay Effective

Skype: rex.jones34
Twitter: @RexJonesII
Email: Rex.Jones@Test4Success.org
LinkedIn: https://www.linkedin.com/in/rexjones34

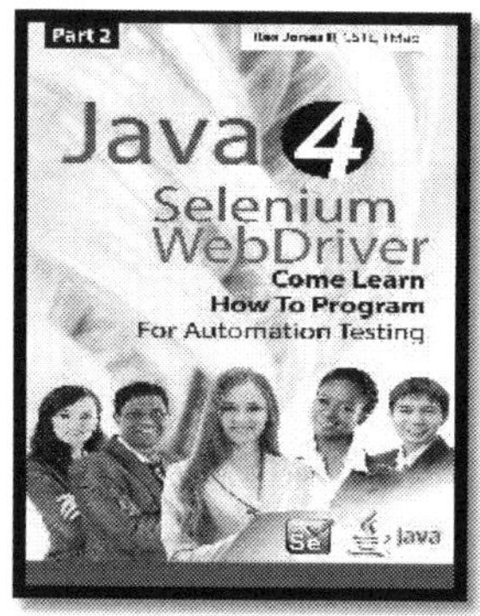

3 Tips To Master QTP/UFT Within 30 Days
http://tinyurl.com/3-Tips-For-QTP-UFT

Free Webinars, Videos, and Live Trainings
http://tinyurl.com/Free-QTP-UFT-Selenium

Sign Up To Receive

1. 3 Tips To Master QTP/UFT Within 30 Days
   http://tinyurl.com/3-Tips-For-QTP-UFT

2. 3 Tips To Master Selenium Within 30 Days
   http://tinyurl.com/3-Tips-For-Selenium

3. Free Webinars, Videos, and Live Trainings
   http://tinyurl.com/Free-QTP-UFT-Selenium

Skype: rex.jones34
Twitter: @RexJonesII
Email: Rex.Jones@Test4Success.org
LinkedIn: https://www.linkedin.com/in/rexjones34

Made in the USA
San Bernardino, CA
28 April 2019

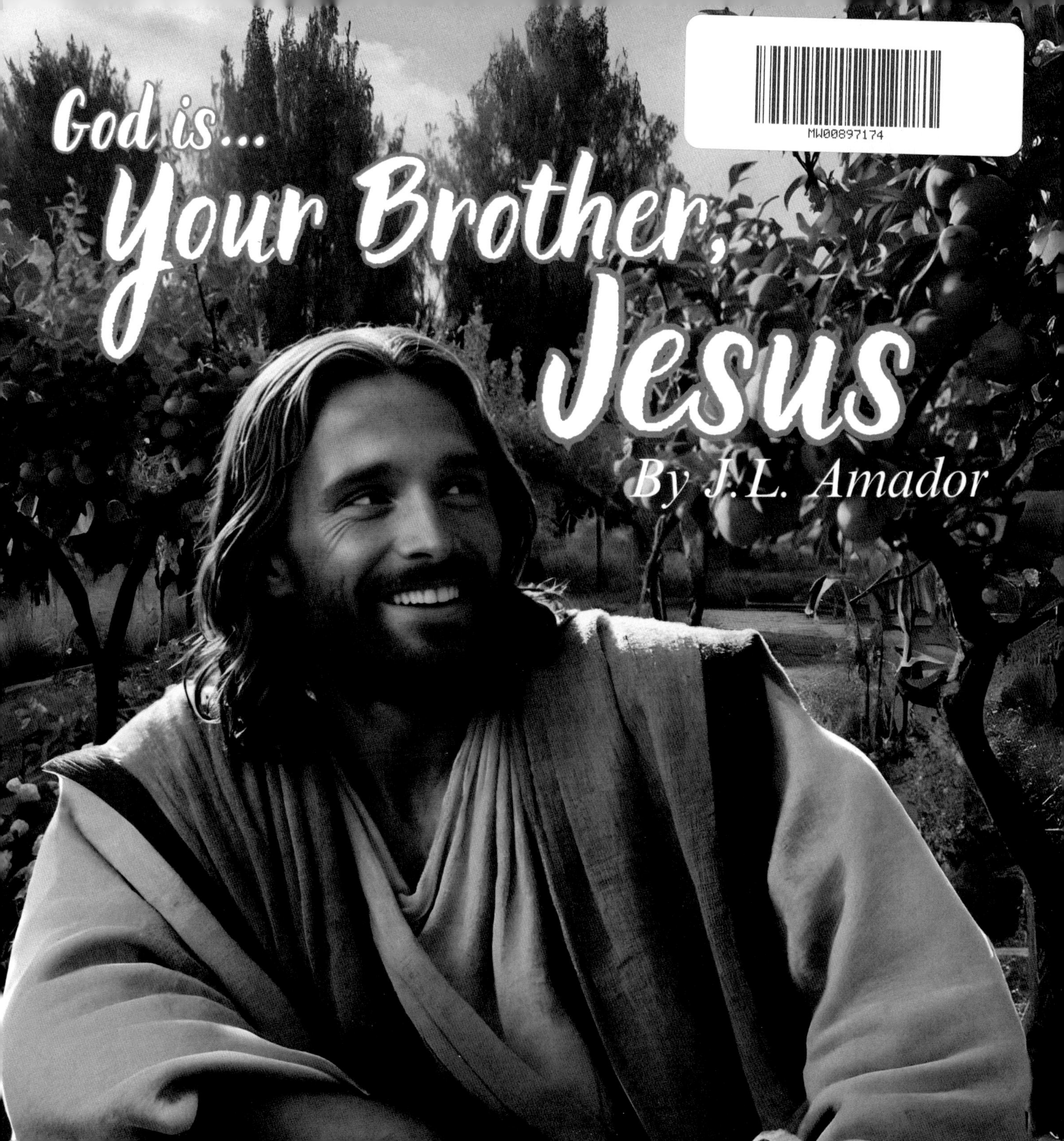
MW00897174
God is...
Your Brother,
Jesus
By J.L. Amador

God is...

Your Brother, Jesus

by J.L. Amador

Copyright © 2024 by J.L. Amador

All rights reserved. No portion of this book may be reproduced—mechanically, electronically, or by any other means, including photocopying—without written permission of the publisher.

ISBN: 9798343348682

Book Cover Designing and Illustrations by J.L. Amador

This book belongs to:

Julie asked her brother Louis, “Who is Jesus Christ?”

Louis explained, “Jesus is God himself!

“*The Father* and *the Holy Spirit* are God, too.
God is all three Persons.

“Long before he was born on earth, Jesus was God.

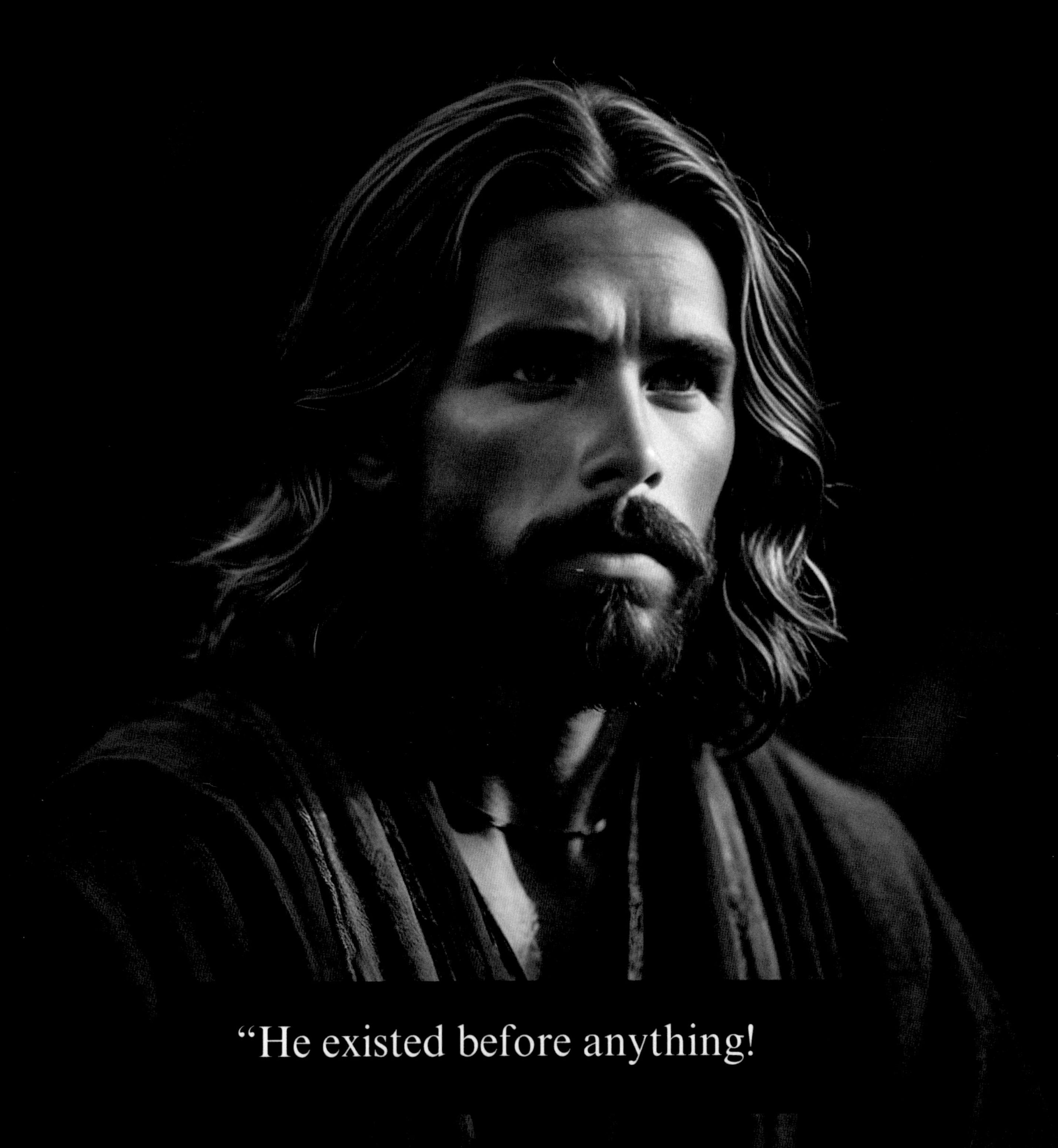

"He existed before anything!

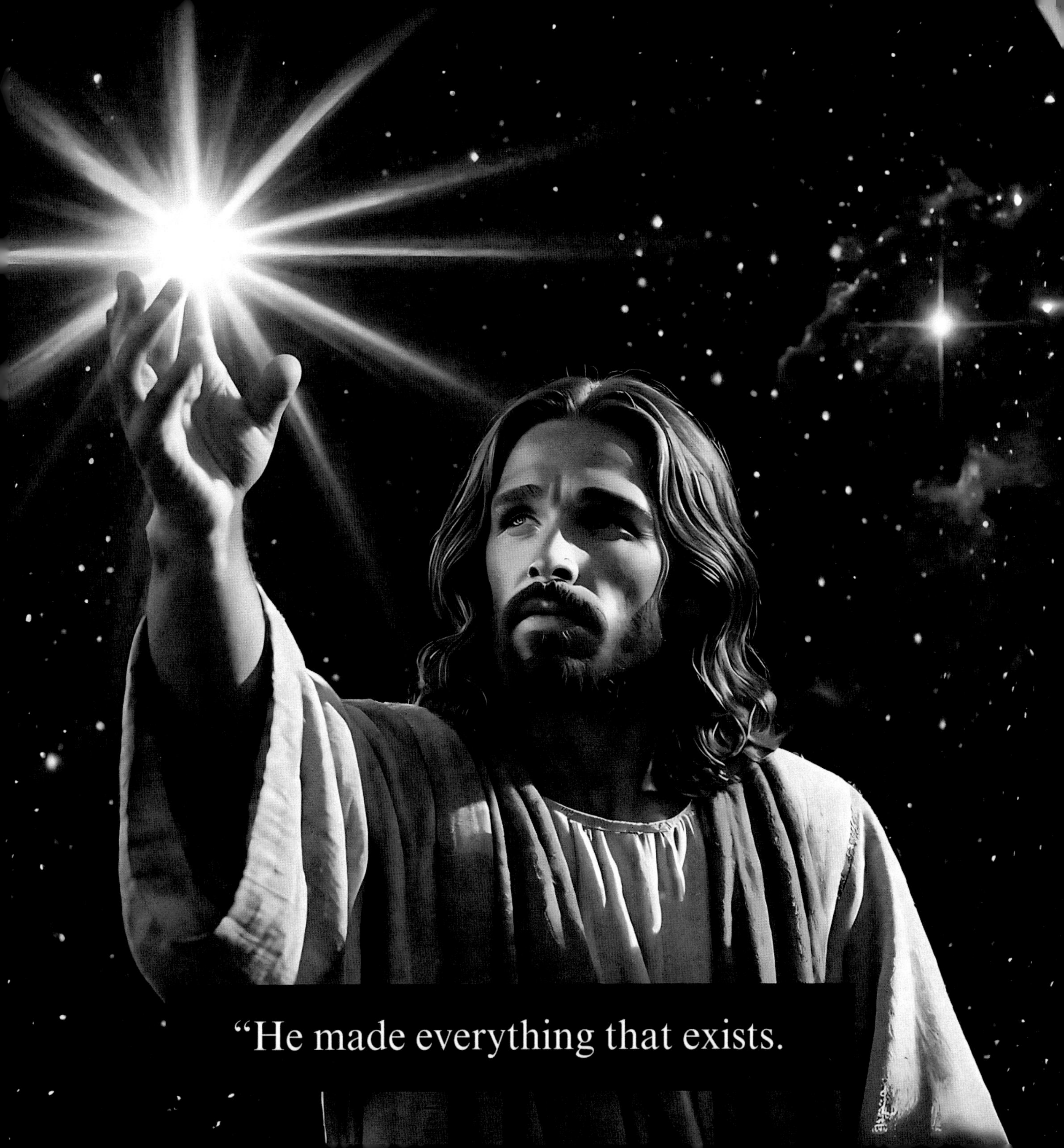

"He made everything that exists.

"God the Father loves us, but we can't get physically close to him, because he embodies the holiness of God.

"Although Jesus is a different person than the Father, their characters are exactly the same. They are described as **one**.

"The Father can remain the Holiness of God,
but he can love us as if we were right close to
him, through Jesus!

“Jesus is called ***the Son of God***, because it best describes how much Jesus is loved by the Father; and we are created God’s children, too!

"The Bible tells us, 'No one has ever seen God. The only Son, **who is the same as God and is at the Father's side**, he has made him known.'

John 1:18 New King James Version

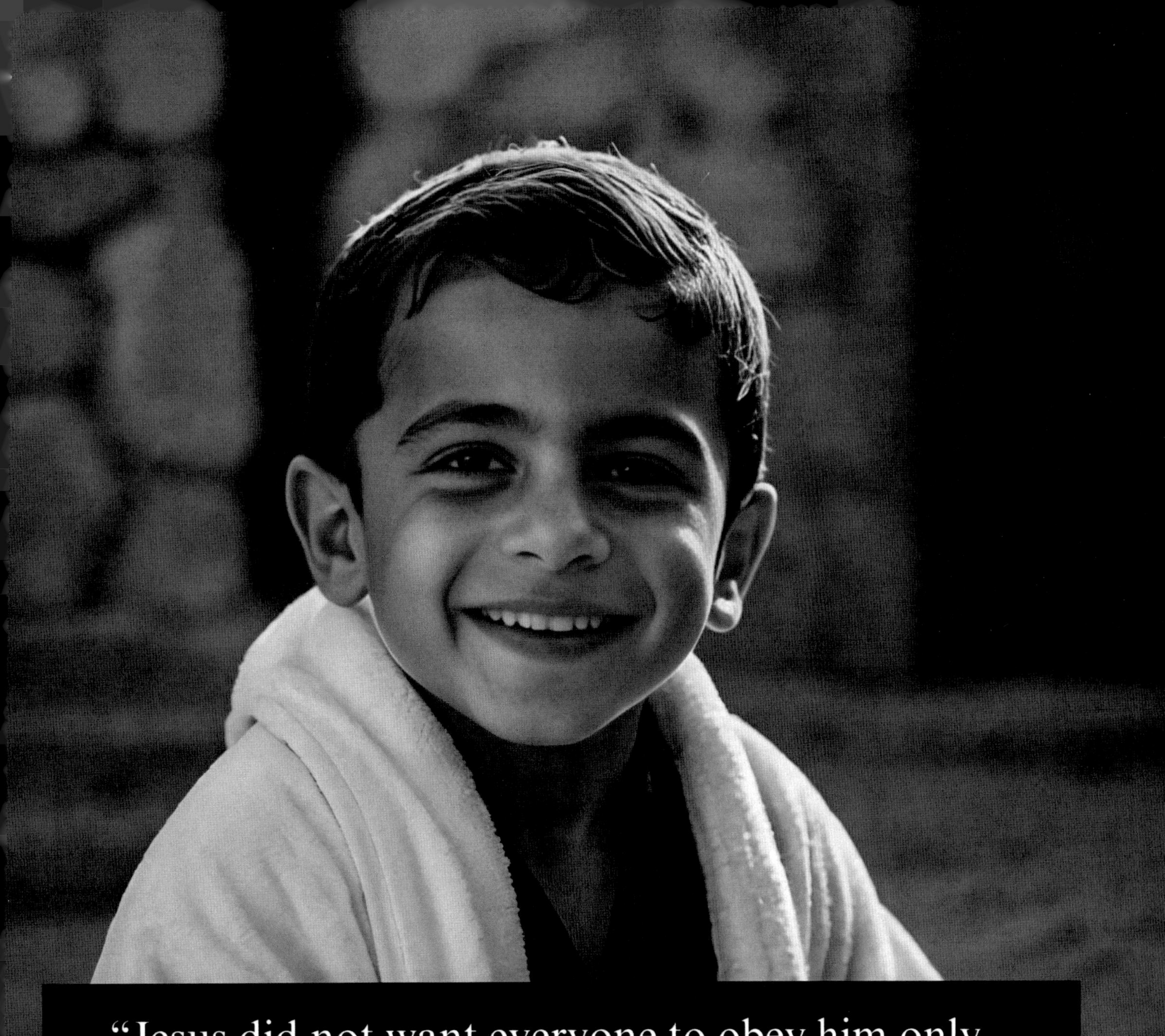

"Jesus did not want everyone to obey him only because he is God, but because we love him. So he became **the child of God** by becoming a human being!

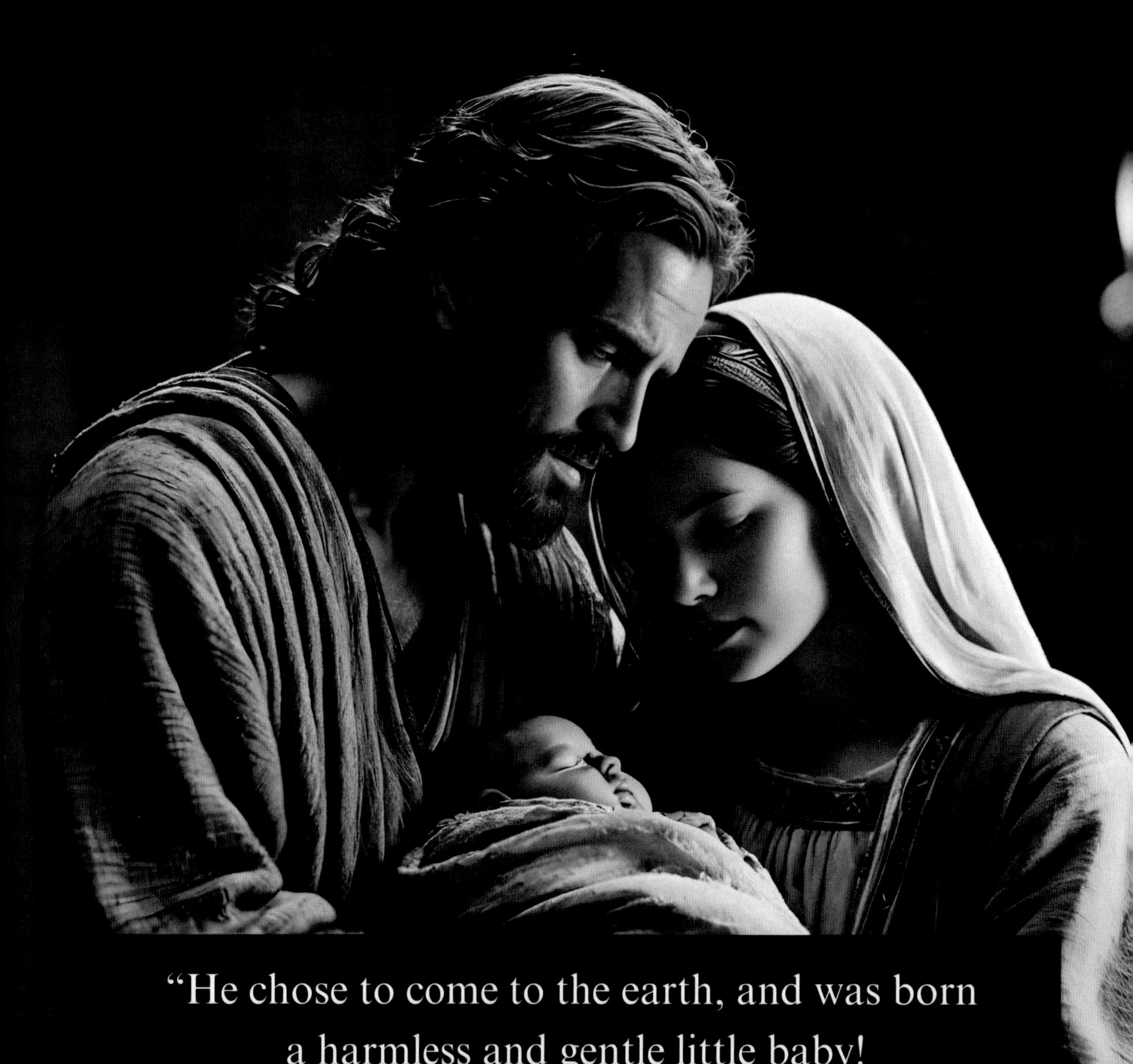

"He chose to come to the earth, and was born
a harmless and gentle little baby!

"Though he had all the power of the universe, he always remained as harmless and gentle all his life.

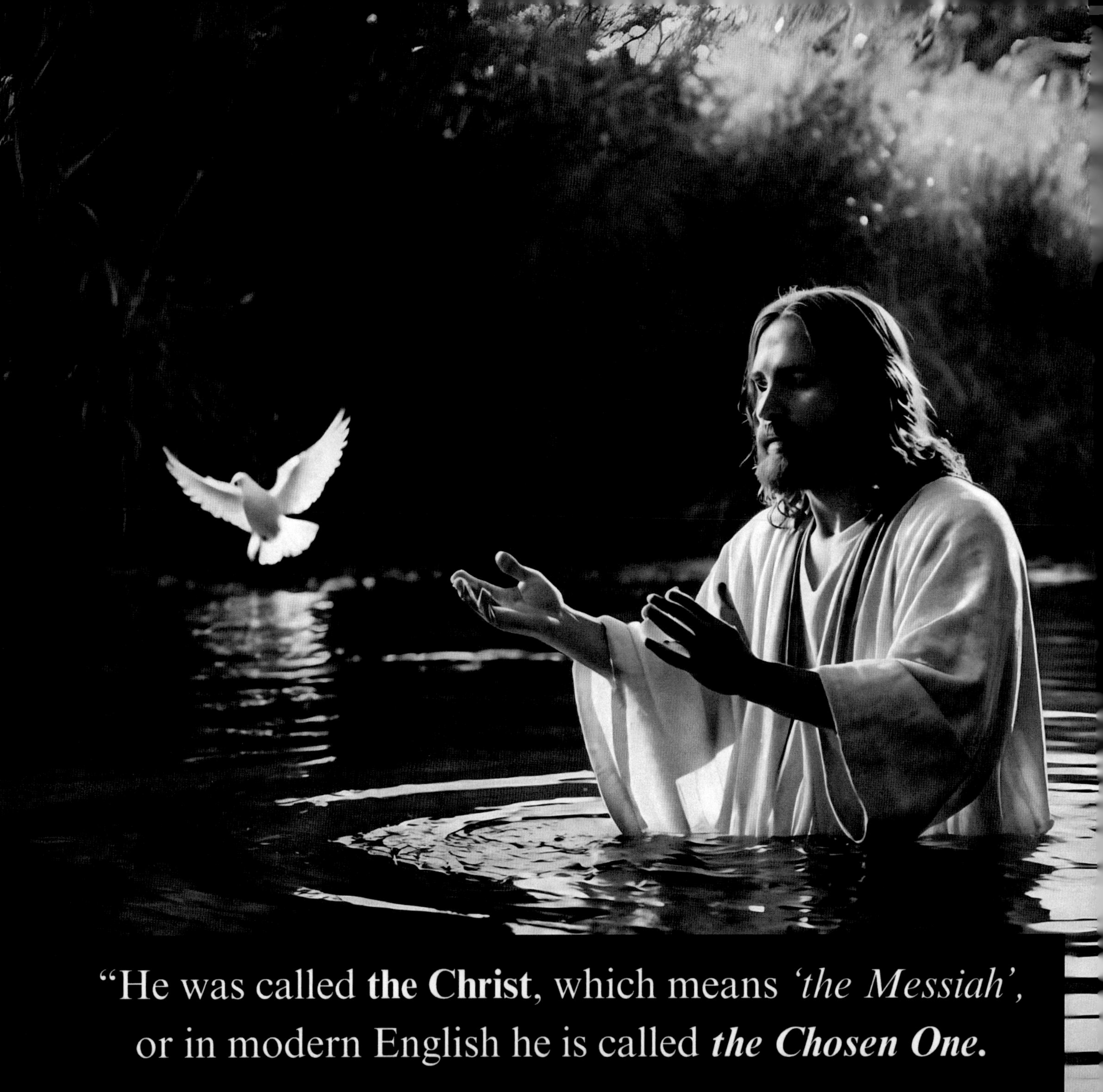

"He was called **the Christ**, which means *'the Messiah'*, or in modern English he is called ***the Chosen One.***

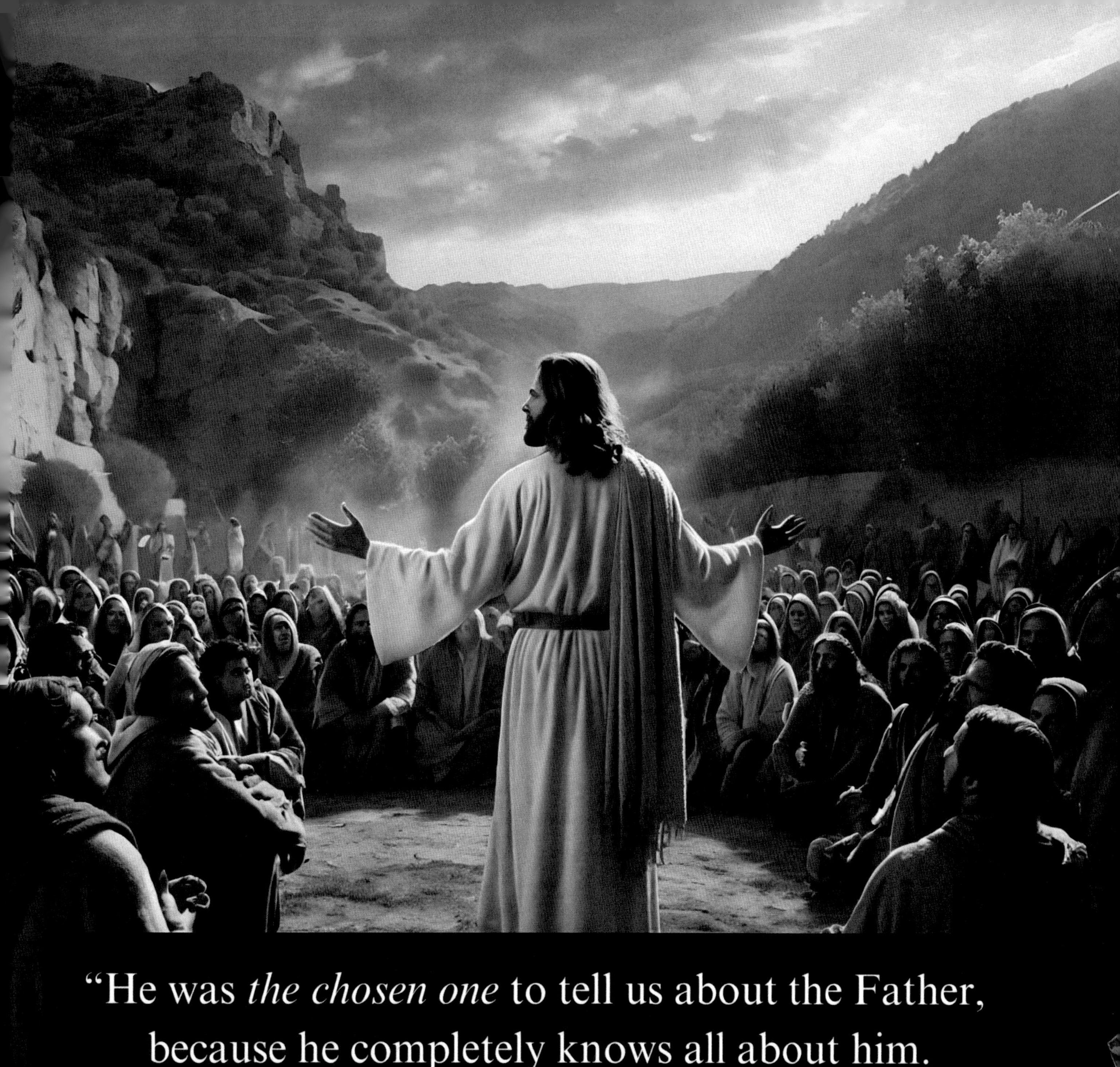

“He was *the chosen one* to tell us about the Father,
because he completely knows all about him.

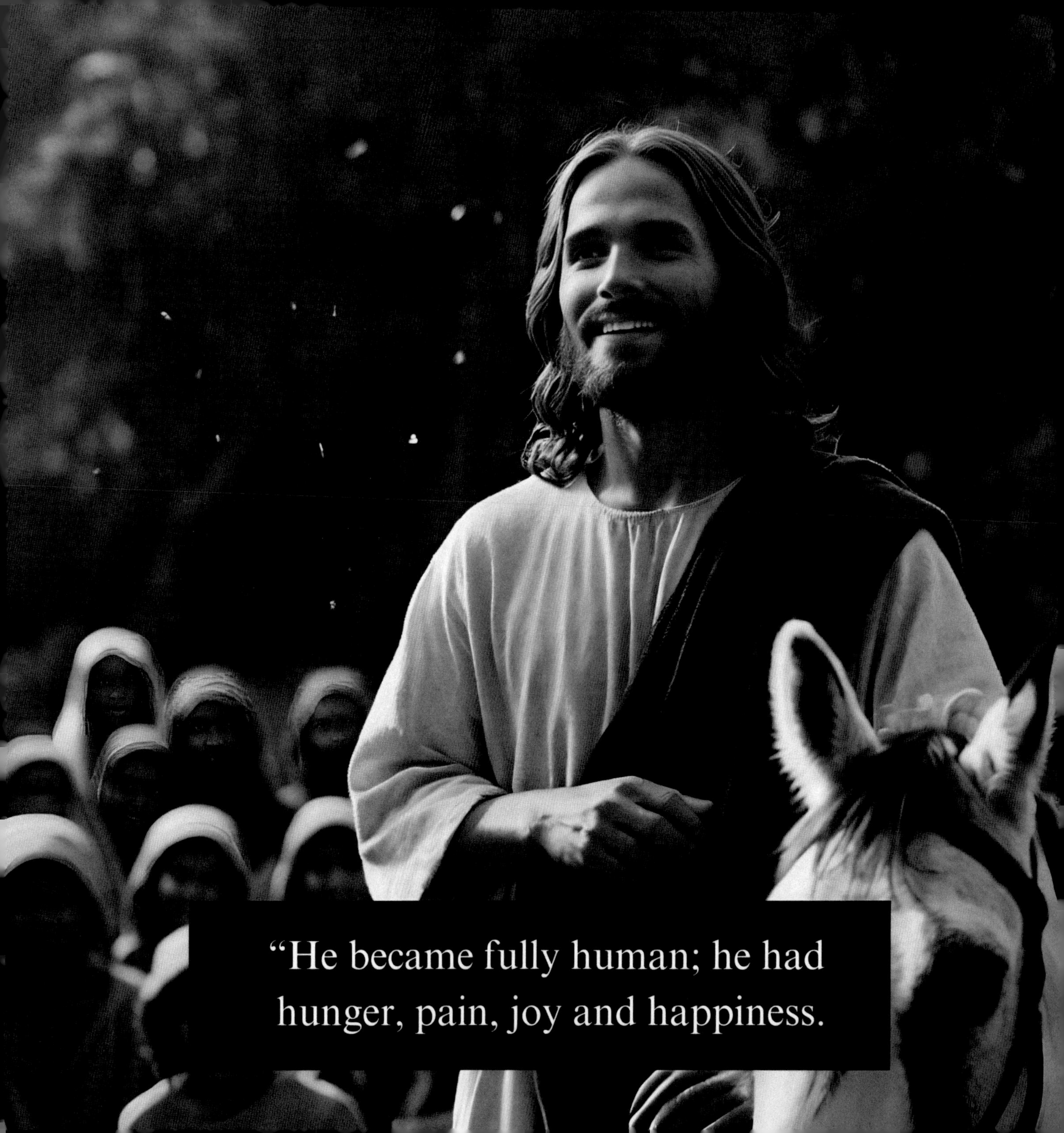
"He became fully human; he had
hunger, pain, joy and happiness.

“Yet he never stopped being God!

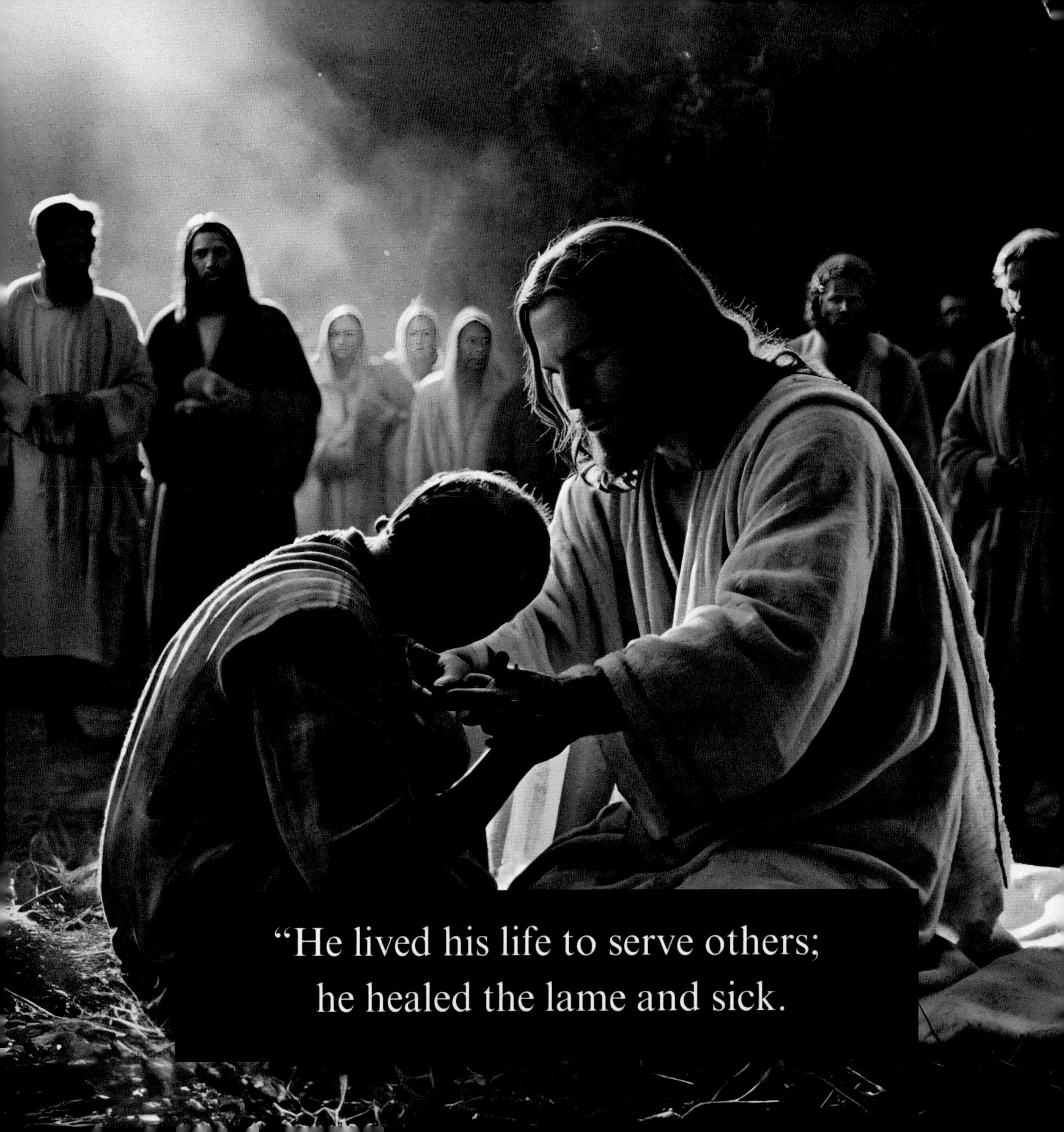
"He lived his life to serve others;
he healed the lame and sick.

"Once he was asked, 'Show us the Father.' Jesus said, 'Have I been with you so long, and you don't know who I am? He that has seen me has seen the Father!'
John 14:9 New King James Version

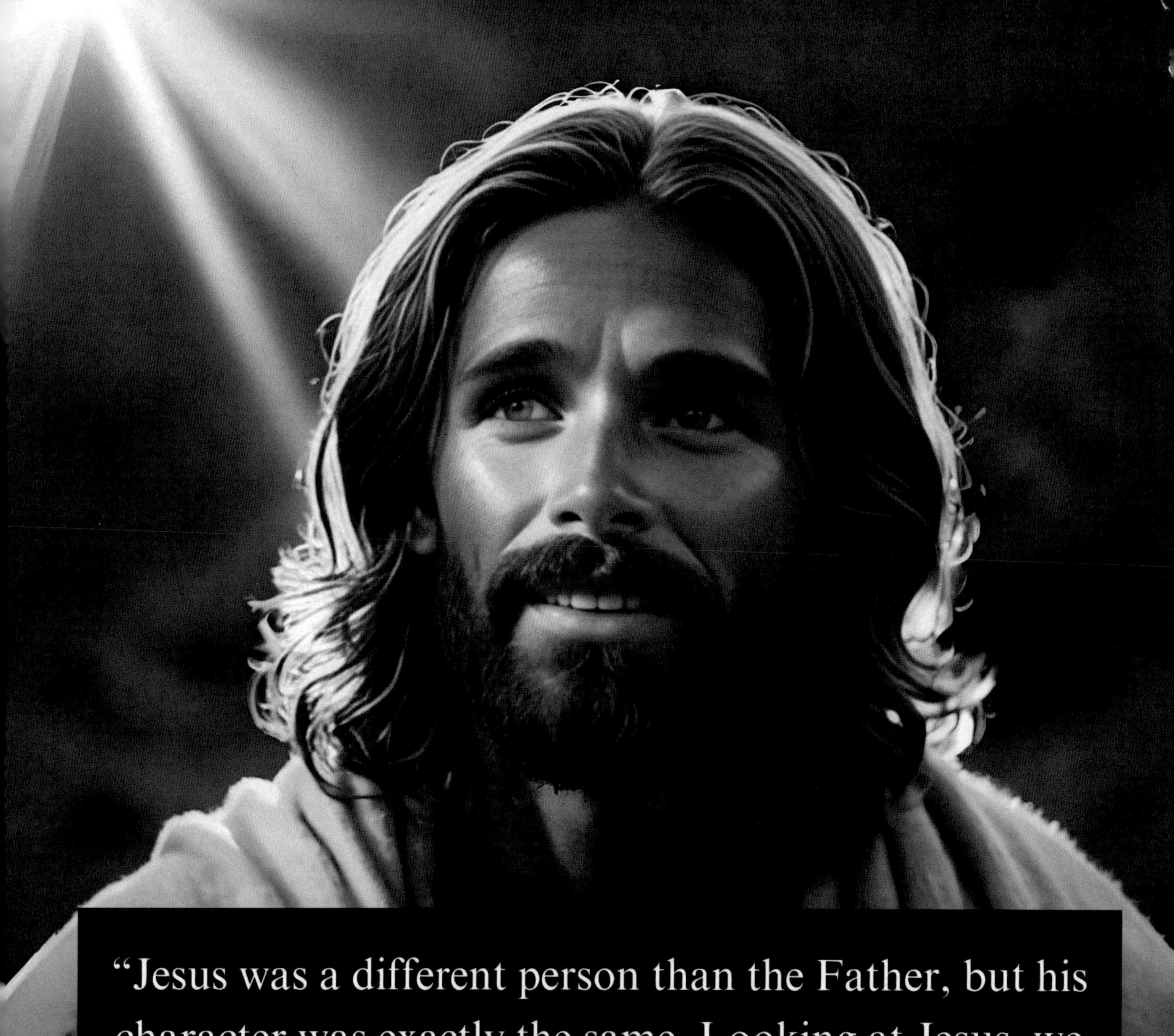

“Jesus was a different person than the Father, but his character was exactly the same. Looking at Jesus, we know that the Father would do the exact same thing.

"He is 100% God, and also 100% human. The Bible says, 'For there is one God, and there is one who brings God and human beings together, **the man** Christ Jesus.'

1 Timothy 2:5 Good News Translation

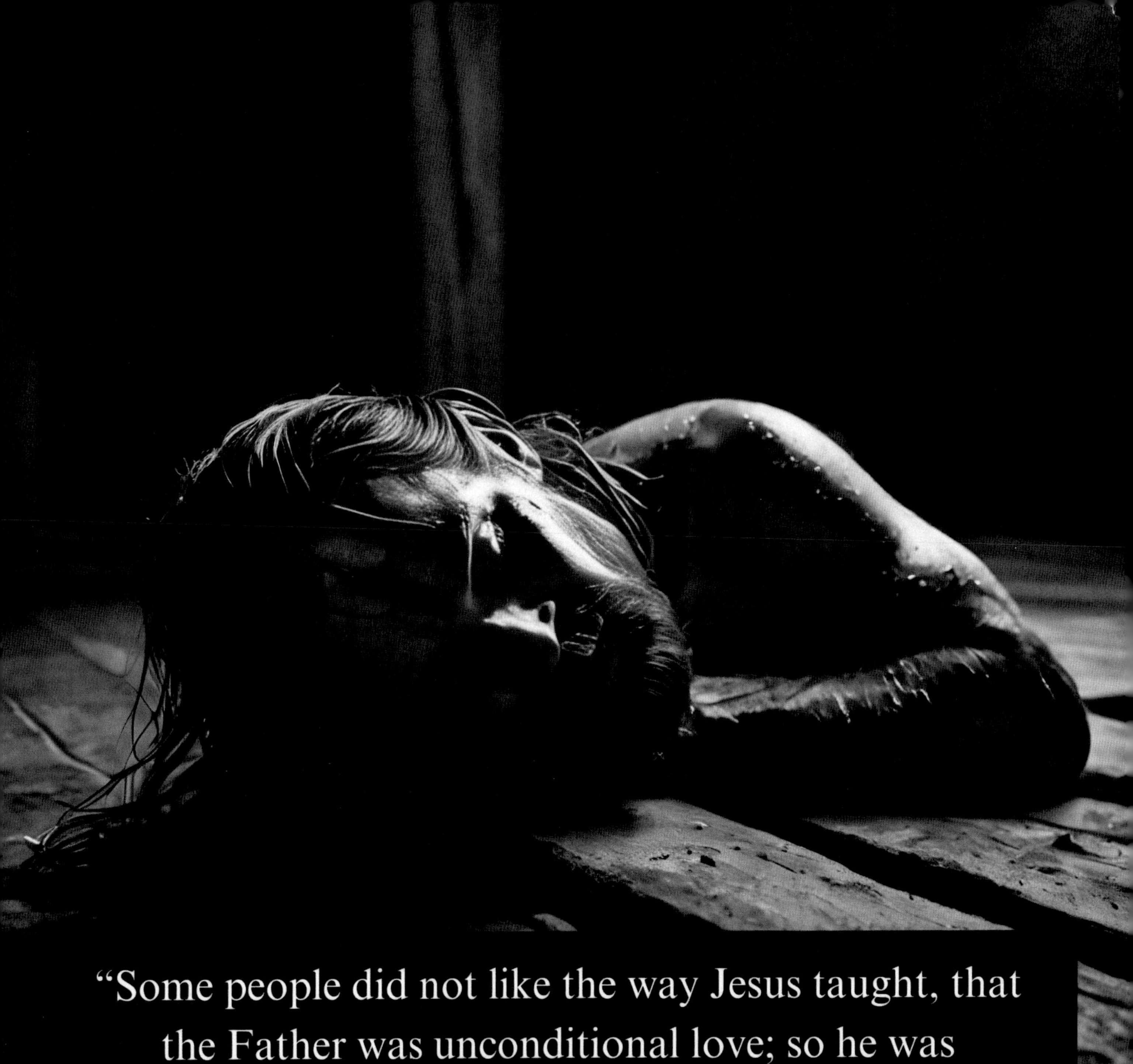

“Some people did not like the way Jesus taught, that the Father was unconditional love; so he was eventually killed by a group of evil people.

“He suffered horrible pain, but it was his **heart** which suffered the most, like no one ever did. His heart was bigger that the universe!

"No one will ever suffer so much, because he is God!

"We deserve to die because of our sins; but although he did not deserve it, he died in our place!

“He was crucified on a wooden cross, to kill him.

"But he had said, 'No one takes it from me, but I lay it down of myself. I have power to lay it down, and I have power to take it again.'

John 10:18 New King James Version

His heart was so filled with sorrow,
he died on the cross.

"But just as he had told many times that he would die for our sin, he also said that three days later, he would come back to life!

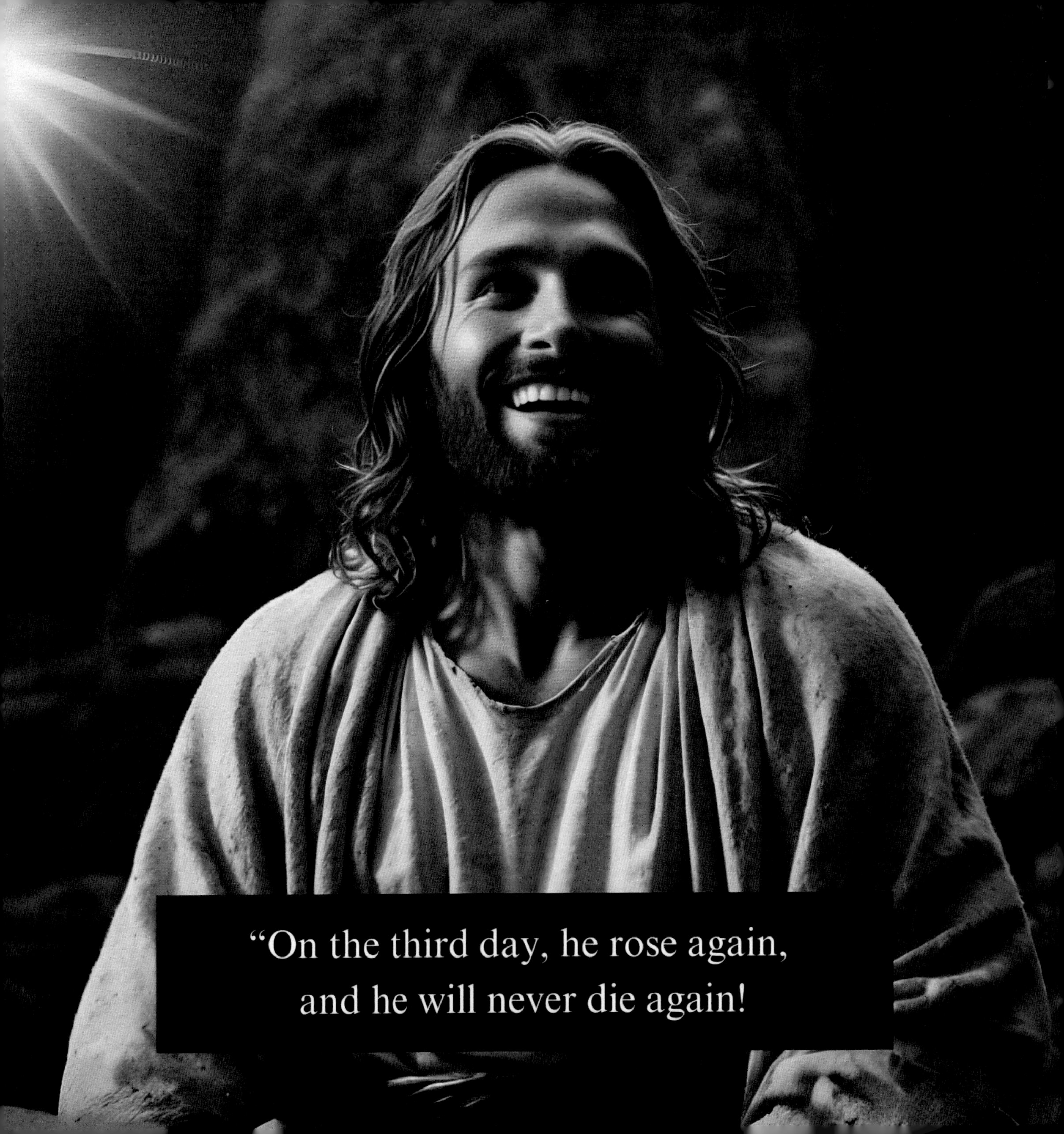
"On the third day, he rose again,
and he will never die again!

“He invites us to live trusting him,
loving him, and obeying him.

"He said that the most important command he has is that *we are to love one another,* like he does!

“He will always be there for you, no matter what!

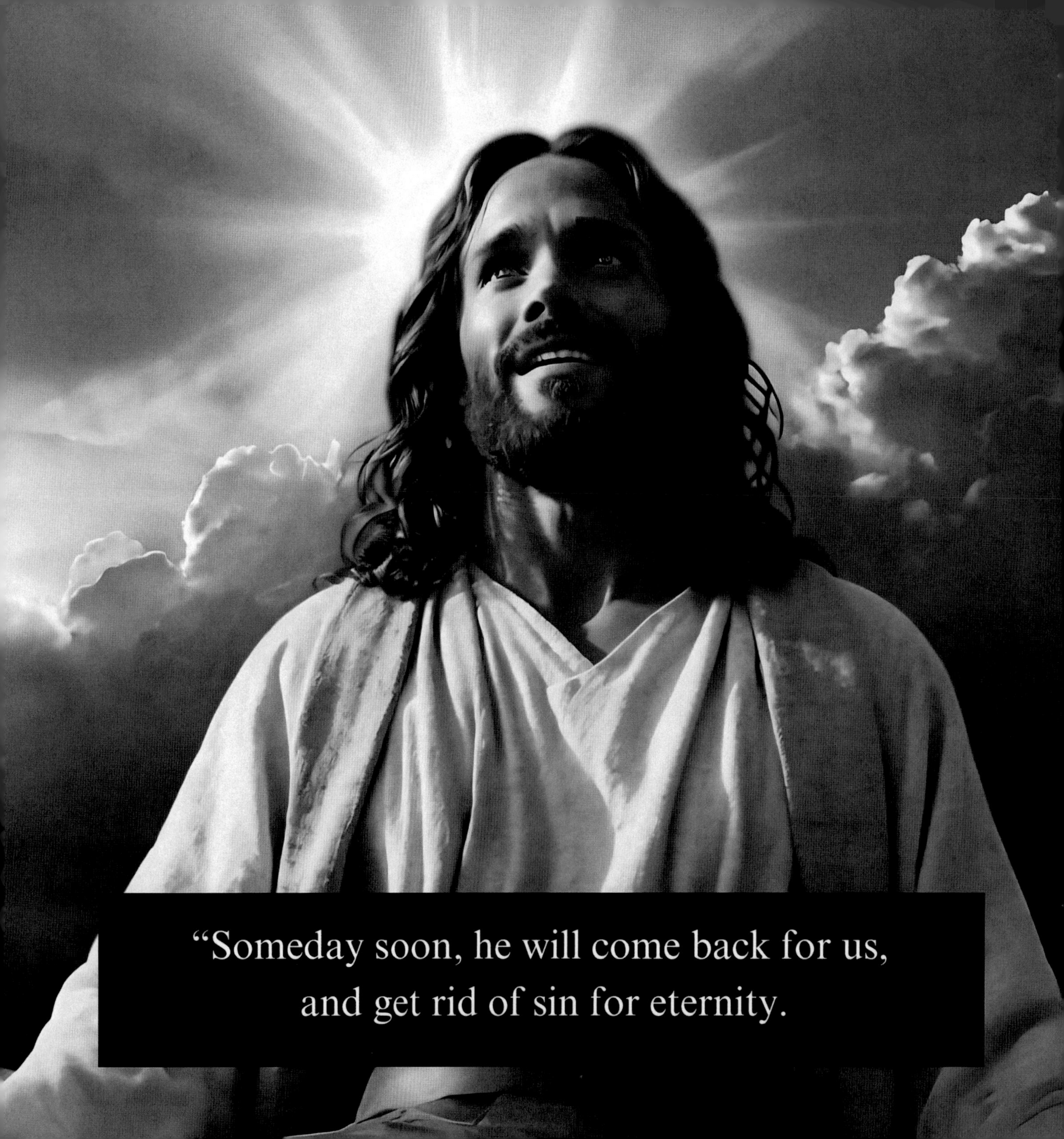
"Someday soon, he will come back for us,
and get rid of sin for eternity.

“He will take us home to Heaven,
and we will forever live with him!”

The End

This set of books was written to help **children** learn about God, the Trinity. You can help promote this book in the following 5 ways:

—Tell all your friends about these books, and tell them to read them
—Tell your Sunday School Class teacher about these books
—Purchase these books as birthday presents or Christmas gifts
—Write to the author and tell him what you think of these books:
J.L. Amador - 390 Mike Loza Dr. #208 - Camarillo, CA 93012
—Read the other books of this series and learn what they teach:

Older people that wish to learn in detail what the Bible teaches on the subject may purchase the following book, available at Amazon.com:

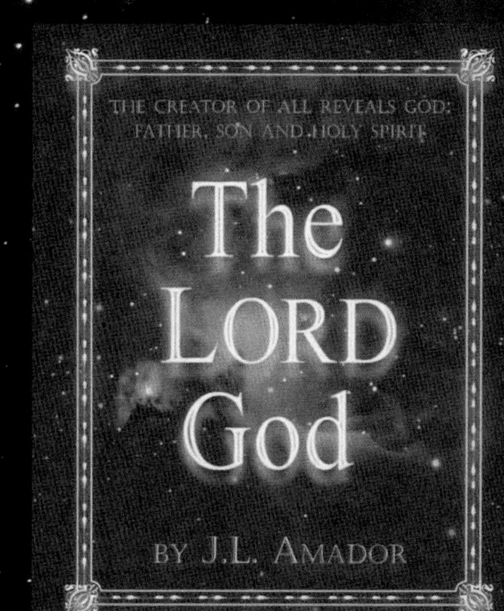

Made in the USA
Middletown, DE
07 November 2024